Doubt and Religious Commitment

DOUBT AND RELIGIOUS COMMITMENT

The Role of the Will in Newman's Thought

M. JAMIE FERREIRA

CLARENDON PRESS · OXFORD
1980

Oxford University Press, Walton Street, Oxford OX2 6DP

OXFORD LONDON GLASGOW
NEW YORK TORONTO MELBOURNE WELLINGTON
KUALA LUMPUR SINGAPORE JAKARTA HONG KONG TOKYO
DELHI BOMBAY CALCUTTA MADRAS KARACHI
NAIROBI DAR ES SALAAM CAPE TOWN

*Published in the United States by
Oxford Univeristy Press, New York*

British Library Cataloguing in Publication Data

Ferreira, M. Jamie
  Doubt and religious commitment.
  1. Newman, John Henry
  2. Faith
  I. Title
  248′.2   BX4705.N5   79-42785
  ISBN 0-19-826654-5

*Set by Hope Services, Abingdon
and Printed in Great Britain by
Billing & Sons Limited,
London, Guildford and Worcester*

Acknowledgements

My deepest debt of gratitude is owed to those members of the Princeton Department of Religion — Victor Preller, Malcolm Diamond, and Jeffrey Stout — under whose wise and generous guidance this project was born. In particular, Victor's availability and patience during one crucial summer of writing were indispensable. Professors James Livingston (College of William and Mary) and James Collins (St. Louis University) also deserve thanks for their thoughtful comments on an early draft. Several of my colleagues here at Yale have been especially kind — William Christian Sr. painstakingly read several versions of the manuscript, offering detailed and perceptive criticism each time; the reading of a near-final version by Gene Outka and Hans Frei resulted in a number of fruitful suggestions, as well as much-appreciated encouragement. In addition, I am grateful to the Council on the Humanities at Yale for providing an A. Whitney Griswold Faculty Research grant for the typing of the manuscript. Finally, I dedicate this book to K. E. Tanner who more than anyone else shared the joys and frustrations that attended its growth.

New Haven September 1979

Contents

Abbreviations

The following abbreviations will be used throughout the text. The dates in parentheses refer to the date of first publication or delivery, followed (where appropriate) by the date of the revised edition. Following the parenthetical dates are the place of publication and date of the edition used in giving references.

Apo.   *Apologia Pro Vita Sua* (1864, ed. 1886), Oxford, 1967.

Dev.   *An Essay on the Development of Christian Doctrine* (1845, ed. 1878), London, 1878.

Ess.   *Essays Critical and Historical* (1828–1846, ed. 1871), Vol. 1, London, 1872.

G.A.   *An Essay in Aid of a Grammar of Assent* (1870), London, 1901.

Idea   *The Idea of a University Defined and Illustrated* (1852–1858, ed. 1873), New York and London, 1960.

L.G.   *Loss and Gain: The Story of a Convert* (1874), London, 1874.

L.D.   *Letters and Diaries of John Henry Newman*, Vols. 11–18 (1845–1858), ed. C. S. Dessain *et. al.*, London, 1961–8.

Mix. I   *Discourses Addresed to Mixed Congregations* (1849), Vol. I, London, 1881.

T.P.   *The Theological Papers of John Henry Newman on Faith and Certainty* (1846–1886), ed. Achaval and Holmes, Oxford, 1976.

U.S.   *Fifteen Sermons Preached Before the University of Oxford* (1826–1843, ed. 1871), London, 1970.

V.M. I   *Via Media of the Anglican Church*, Vol. I: *Lectures on the Prophetical Office of the Church, Viewed Relatively to Romanism and Popular Protestantism* (1837, ed. 1877), London, 1911.

Ward II   Wilfred Ward, *The Life of John Henry Cardinal Newman*, Vol. II, London, 1912.

Harper   Gordon Huntington Harper (ed.), *Cardinal Newman and William Froude, FRS: A Correspondence*, Baltimore, 1933.

Introduction

> There is faith in every serious doubt ... he who
> seriously denies God, affirms him ... there is no
> possible atheism.
>
> Paul Tillich, *The Protestant Era*

> The role of theism in Victorian life was conflict-
> creating; that role is lost now. ... The theism in
> which Feuerbach disbelieved underwent a sea change
> into the theism in which Tillich believed.
>
> Alasdair MacIntyre, *The Religious*
> *Significance of Atheism*

In a very simple and pointed question addressed to a high-
ranking Victorian cleric, John Henry Newman highlighted a
problem which has long troubled reflective religious believers,
a problem raised as often in the depths of their own hearts
as by external critics. 'Then pray', Newman asked, 'what is
the difference between Faith and Prejudice?'[1] In these words
Newman revealed the tension he saw between the kind of
adherence necessary for religious devotion and the kind of
adherence legitimate for a rational believer. In its more
general form the difficulty on which Newman focused is the
following: Religious commitment must be *unconditional* —
what kind of adherence is therefore both adequate and
legitimate? A vast contemporary literature is dedicated to the
question of what constitutes genuine religious commitment.
Countless articles carrying on long-lived debates between
opposing parties testify to the importance of the problem
today to those who attempt to appraise sensitively and
critically the relevance of philosophy to religion.[2] Among
the questions raised are the following: Is some form of

[1] Ward II, p. 245.
[2] I refer to the discussion from Antony Flew's challenge in the fifties to the
present. The articles are too numerous to mention, but the authors I find most
helpful are the following: R. M. Hare, Basil Mitchell, Kai Nielsen, W. D. Hudson,
William Austin, Ian Barbour, Alasdair MacIntyre, D. Z. Phillips, Diogenes
Allen, Norman Malcolm, Peter Winch, Ian Crombie, and Patrick Sherry.

immunity to criticism a necessary feature of 'unconditional' commitment? Is some form of susceptibility to criticism (which for convenience I will call 'criticizability') a necessary feature of rational commitment? In this way Newman's concern remains a vital one.

Newman's understanding of the 'unconditionality' of faith centred on the claim that faith and doubt 'cannot co-exist'.[3] Rational justification, however, was a legitimate demand. The tension between passionate, enduring devotedness and rational adherence could be maintained, Newman argued, without requiring the denial of the claim that 'faith is incompatible with doubt'.[4] This answer stands in sharp contrast to a variety of significant modern positions on the relation between religious commitment and doubt. These positions differ markedly among themselves, and a brief survey of their variety, while unable to do justice to any single position, will at least suggest the complexity of the problem.

One important tradition in religious thought claims that doubt is compatible with, perhaps necessary to, religious commitment. This claim comes from two main directions. In some cases the claim has 'existentialist' underpinnings, denying or downplaying the appropriateness or need of rational justification. Paul Tillich's emphases on autonomy and self-involvement, for example, inform his claim that 'serious doubt is confirmation of faith' and that faith can 'include the doubt about itself'.[5] Tillich takes two approaches to the question, both resulting in a requirement of 'existential' doubt. First, doubt is a necessary structural element in faith because otherwise autonomy could not be preserved; we must always see the concrete content of our ultimate concern as non-definitive, and open to criticism. Because doubt must be maintained in this way, a propositional element in faith cannot be crucial since 'if faith is understood as belief that something is true, doubt is incompatible with the act of faith'.[6] Secondly, the personal certitude of faith must not be able to be undercut by experience. Since beliefs that something is the case do not yield complete certitude in this

---

[3] *V.M. I*, p. 87, n. 2 (1872 emendation).
[4] *Mix.*, p. 216.
[5] *Dynamics of Faith* (New York: Harper Torchbooks, 1957), p. 22; p. 20.
[6] Ibid., p. 18.

respect, the certitude of faith cannot attach to such theoretical beliefs.[7] Since faith does not depend on theoretical beliefs, doubt can be compatible. The assumption of theologians like Tillich is that a shift away from rational justification is necessary because adequate critical autonomy and a personal certainty that cannot be undercut by experience are impossible without such a shift. Once such a shift is made, a non-propositional doubt is integrated into the concept of faith.[8]

In other cases, however, the claim that religious commitment is compatible with doubt is the result of affirming the need and appropriateness of rational justification of religious belief. According to such accounts, since criticism and rational argumentation must be possible with respect to religious commitment, we must be able to doubt intellectually while remaining genuinely committed. For this reason Roger Trigg, in *Reason and Commitment,* claims that 'questioning my beliefs and even doubting their truth need not necessarily weaken my commitment'.[9] From both directions and for a variety of reasons, therefore, the possibility of critical, free commitment is said to require the compatibility of doubt and religious commitment.

An equally important tradition, on the other hand, finds doubt incompatible with faith. For some of these writers it is precisely because criticizability is unacceptable. Religious commitment must transcend categories of rational justification if it is not to be undermined by the criticism which is the obverse of such justification. Reasons cannot be relevant to faith because either too much or too little conviction would thereby be generated; either the freedom of faith would be prejudiced or the 'unconditional' passionate adherence of faith would be jeopardized.[10] In this case, free

---

[7] Ibid., pp. 34–5.

[8] As exemplified in Tillich's introduction to *The Protestant Era* (Chicago: University of Chicago Press, 1957 (abr. ed.)), pp. x, xi.

[9] Cambridge: At the University Press, 1973, p. 46. A similar idea is found in Ian Barbour's book, *Myths, Models and Paradigms* (New York: Harper & Row, 1974), pp. 179–80.

[10] The clearest example is found in the early piece by Alasdair MacIntyre, 'The Logical Status of Religious Belief', in *Metaphysical Beliefs*, ed. MacIntyre (London: SCM Press, 1957). The same idea can be found in Rudolf Bultmann's *Jesus Christ and Mythology* (New York: Scribner's, 1958), and *Kerygma and Myth,* ed. Hans Werner Bartsch (New York: Harper Torchbooks, 1961), pp. 191–211.

passionate adherence is said to require the incompatibility, rather than the compatibility, of doubt. Like Tillich, they agree that the certitude of faith cannot be allowed to be undercut by experience, but their conclusion is that the criticizability which Tillich ultimately tries to guarantee is incompatible with religious commitment. Once again the result is a turn away from propositional commitment to 'personal' commitment, but the turn is at the same time a turn away from critical commitment. Critical commitment cannot, it is said, be adequately religious. Faith is, instead, a matter of finding ourselves at a place in life where we worship — religious belief cannot be justified except by 'faith'.[11] Rational justification and the doubt that links up with it are incompatible with the demands of religious devotion.

In the tradition of those who find doubt incompatible, however, we find some who nevertheless see the shift away from rational justification as a disservice to religion, and an unnecessary disservice at that. Newman, for example, repeatedly asserts the importance of rational justification — we must have *'reason enough* to resolve to place faith'.[12] He considers it 'undeniable' that

Reason has a power of analysis and criticism in all opinion and conduct, and that nothing is true or right but what may be justified, and in a certain sense, proved by it, and undeniable, in consequence, that unless the doctrines received by Faith are approvable by Reason, they have no claim to be regarded as true.[13]

None the less he holds that faith and doubt are incompatible. His position, therefore, differs from those described above with respect to the relation between doubt and religious commitment and/or the relation between rational justification and religious commitment.

It should be clear now that discussions of the character of religious commitment and its relation to doubt involve an interesting set of possible cross-combinations. The claim that

[11] D. Z. Phillips and Norman Malcolm could be said to be the best proponents of this view.

[12] Harper, p. 91 (20 Oct. 1851).

[13] *U.S.,* X, p. 182. Throughout Sermons X–XIV Newman claims either that it is necessary that faith be justified by reason, or at least that such justification would not be inappropriate. Either claim is sufficient to distinguish him from 'Wittgensteinian fideists'.

faith and doubt are *compatible* can be supported by reference to the need for rational justification as well as by a devaluation of that need. The claim that faith and doubt are *incompatible* can be tied either to a claim that rational justification is appropriate or to a claim that religion transcends categories of rationality. In addition there are more subtle variations on these themes. For example, we find the claim that one kind of doubt is incompatible, but that another kind is compatible,[14] as well as the claim that the dangerous threat constituted by a particular kind of doubt is to be striven against but is nevertheless inevitable in our situation as fallen pilgrims seeking God.[15] The question raised by such a variety of positions on the relation between religious commitment and doubt is: what kind of doubt is being judged, in each historical context, to be compatible or incompatible with religious commitment, and why?

The implications of this question for the problem of religious commitment concern the following general questions:

(1) what kind of doubt can be compatible with religious commitment while doing justice to the 'unconditional' character of commitment;

(2) how does the kind of doubt in a compatibility claim depend on the position on rational justification allied to it;

(3) what kind of doubt can be incompatible with religious commitment and yet do justice to the risk-taking and free surrender of religious commitment;

(4) what kind of doubt can be incompatible and yet consistent with an admission of the relevance and necessity of rational justification?

These questions, however, can only be addressed if we ask of separate historical accounts of religious commitment precisely what kind of doubt is being assumed in the discussion. In particular we need to determine each account's *descriptive*

[14] W. D. Hudson, 'Professor Bartley's Theory of Rationality and Religious Belief', *Religious Studies* 9 (Sept. 1973).

[15] Karl Barth, *Evangelical Theology: An Introduction,* trans. Grover Foley (New York: Holt, Rinehart & Winston, 1963), pp. 121–32. Barth criticizes Tillich in this respect, arguing that we ought to be ashamed of our doubt, not celebrate it.

and *prescriptive* understanding of the relation between doubt and commitment, as well as the implication of the prescriptive understanding for the possibility of *criticizability*. Final judgements of differences and similarities between accounts are impossible without such preliminary determinations; such preliminary determinations are also indispensable to any constructive approach to the problem of religious commitment.

The contrast between Newman's Roman Catholic claim about the relation between religious commitment, doubt, and rational justification and contemporary claims about that relation seems to parallel a comparison of the Victorian age with our own made by Alasdair MacIntyre. MacIntyre suggests that contemporary theologians, in attempting to lessen the tension between theism and secular culture, have 'emptied [Christianity] of any content that might affront us culturally'.[16] They have been over successful in eliminating the conflict-creating role of Christianity in the Victorian age — an age where faith made demands because it had a content. Emasculation of vital religion, ostensibly in the name of vital religion, occurs, MacIntyre suggests, where 'relevance' is equated with 'compatibility'. The result is that some contemporary theologizing constitutes a psychological reduction of theism which is 'exactly what was called atheism in the nineteenth century'.[17]

Whether or not MacIntyre's diatribes against contemporary theology are well-founded in general,[18] his analysis is suggestive with respect to the question of the compatibility of faith and doubt. The theologizing he criticizes as lacking in content is very often the theologizing like Tillich's which makes faith and doubt compatible, theologizing for which 'there is no possible atheism'. Not all the theologizing that makes faith and doubt compatible has such drastic con-

---

[16] 'The Debate About God: Victorian Relevance and Contemporary Irrelevance', *The Religious Significance of Atheism*, Bampton Lectures (New York and London: Columbia University Press, 1969), pp. 20–1.
[17] Ibid., pp. 27–8.
[18] For criticisms of MacIntyre's line of attack, see 'Honesty and Commitment: A Philosopher's View' by Henry Aiken, and 'Unconscious Intellectual Dishonesty in Religion' by William Alston; both are found in *Intellectual Honesty and Religious Commitment*, ed. Arthur Bellinzoni and Thomas Litzenburg (Philadelphia: Fortress Press, 1969).

sequences, but MacIntyre's analysis nevertheless leads one to ask whether the equation, implicitly made by some theologians, of the 'possibility of free, passionate or critical commitment' with the 'compatibility of doubt' might resemble in some respects the equation of 'relevance' with 'compatibility' in general. Whatever our conclusion in this regard, it seems clear that there is a strong need to examine the kind of doubt being allowed or proscribed in individual accounts.

I therefore propose to address the problem of religious commitment by examining in detail the account of doubt, certitude, and commitment offered by John Henry Newman in the latter half of the nineteenth century. Newman's account seems especially promising for a number of reasons. First, he devotes a great deal of time and energy to *analysis*. He is far more concerned to analyse the character of religious adherence than many theologians are, and at least as anxious to analyse it as are modern philosophers of religion. Moreover, he is concerned with the relevance of psychology to philosophical conclusions.

Second, and more importantly, Newman attempts to reconcile aspects of very different positions on commitment. For example, in attempting to distinguish faith and prejudice he points to the illegitimacy of total immunity to criticism. Yet he upholds the incompatibility of doubt and commitment. Analysis of how he combines these two positions — separated by other thinkers — can be helpful in determining the relation between different senses of 'doubt' and the possibility of criticism. In addition, he clearly shares existentialist concerns about freedom and passionate self-involvement,[19] while maintaining that doubt is incompatible with commitment. Study of his proposal can perhaps reveal ways in which different senses of 'doubt' can be related to 'free decision'. Moreover, Newman affirms the 'unconditionality' of commitment, but considers it illegitimate to secure

[19] For a consideration of Newman's relation to the Romantic tradition, see the following: Harold Weatherby, *Cardinal Newman in His Age* (Nashville: Vanderbilt University Press, 1973); John Beer, 'Newman and the Romantic Sensibility', in *The English Mind*, ed. Hugh S. Davies and George Watson (Cambridge: University Press, 1964), pp. 193–218; John Coulson, *Newman and the Common Tradition* (Oxford: Clarendon Press, 1970).

this at the cost of transcending categories of rational justification. Newman once observed that 'the *difficulty* is this:—
Faith is conceived to be inconsistent with *doubt*. How then
can it be the result of *reasoning*? since no reasoning in
moral subjects, leads to an indubitable conclusion'.[20] What
Newman saw as a 'difficulty' has been seen by others as an
impossibility. Against those who argue that the relevance of
rational justification would preclude the necessary 'absoluteness' of religious belief, Newman responds with a reinter-
pretation of the limits and extents of reasoning which can
perhaps serve as a corrective to the uncritical (and perhaps
unwitting) assimilation, on the part of some theologians, of a
model of reasoning and certitude which precludes the
possibility of the features they find necessary to religious
belief. Precisely for this reason an analysis of Newman's
understanding of religious commitment can be of special
value in appraising a number of contemporary proposals concerning the inadequacy and irrelevance of 'reasons' — especially
those controversies over 'Wittgensteinian fideism'.[21]

Finally, Newman was aware of reasons for accepting a
claim that faith and doubt are compatible. His claim that
'faith may follow after doubt . . . but the two cannot co-
exist'[22] was, interestingly, made by Newman as a Roman
Catholic emendation of his Anglican claim made forty years
earlier that 'fear', 'despondency', and 'doubt' were *not* inconsistent with faith. He clearly saw a need at the later date for
a different understanding, or at least a different formulation,
of the relation between faith and doubt. For all these reasons
my hope is that a reconsideration of Newman's model of
religious adherence and its relation to doubt can be used to
clarify certain important aspects of general claims about the
relation between doubt and faith, thus contributing to the
contemporary discussion of the character and implications

---

[20] 'Ultimate Resolution of Certainty of Faith' (Easter, 1848), cited in
Appendix III of David Pailin's *The Way to Faith: An Examination of Newman's
'Grammar of Assent' as a Response to the Search for Certainty in Faith* (London:
Epworth Press, 1969), p. 206.

[21] In particular, discussions by D. Z. Phillips, Kai Nielsen, W. D. Hudson,
Diogenes Allen, and Patrick Sherry.

[22] Footnote 2, p. 87, *V.M. I,* emendation of text p. 87.

of religious commitment.

My examination of Newman's account will focus on the description, prescription and criticizability implied in the claim that faith and doubt are incompatible. However, it is crucial to consider as well another claim which is central to Newman's understanding of the relation between doubt and religious commitment — namely, the claim that certitude is an act of the will. Misunderstandings of the claim about doubt are often, though not always, the result of misunderstandings of the claim concerning certitude and the will. Both claims, moreover, bear directly on the contemporary philosophy of religion discussion of commitment, as well as on topics of general interest to philosophy. The two claims I shall be examining in the following essay, therefore, are (1) that certitude is a free act which depends on the will and (2) that doubt is incompatible with the certitude necessary to genuine religious commitment.

Certitude, as we shall see, is a complex act in which rational grounds, assurance and persistence are said to be related.[23] I shall consider in detail the role of the *will* in relation to both the assurance and the persistence Newman sees as necessary for genuine religious commitment. Newman's various descriptions of the free act of certitude have given rise to a number of conflicting interpretations of the status of certitude in his account, and thus of the character of the religious adherence he prescribes. I shall be arguing that Newman's understanding of the relation between willing and certitude involves two different roles of the will — the role of the will in reaching certitude and the role of the will in confirming an experienced certitude. 'Choice' is relevant only to the second; when these two roles are misunderstood or fail to be distinguished, justice cannot be done to Newman's thought.

Newman's two roles of the will effectively distinguish between two kinds of commitment — a non-deliberate passive adherence and a deliberate active adherence. In addition, Newman's conclusions about certainty presaged significant philosophical shifts in the twentieth century concerning the

---

[23] *G.A.*, pp. 216, 258.

epistemological validity of 'personal' reasoning and concerning claims about 'objectivity'. In both these ways Newman contributes to the contemporary discussion of the character of adequate and legitimate religious adherence.

Determination of Newman's position of the 'free act' of certitude will also have a bearing on a long-standing philosophical discussion of the 'will to believe'. Philosophers have rightly pointed out the impossibility of creating belief by an act of will or instantaneous *fiat*; by extension they have undermined the claim that belief can be created by such a *fiat* in response to 'duty'. However, their analyses of belief may have swung the pendulum to an equally unacceptable extreme. H. H. Price, for example, writes that 'deciding that *p* is not a free choice at all, but a forced one'.[24] Louis Pojman, following Bernard Williams, recently argued that since belief aims at truth, 'belief as a judgement is not an act but a *happening*'.[25] Such a judgement or assent to a conclusion is 'an automatic nod caused by factors not directly in the control of the subject'; belief is 'involuntary' — 'once the objective factors are recognized, the assent comes automatically, of itself'.[26] Newman's work raises the possibility of different senses of 'decision', with different relations to freedom, compulsion, and constraint. I suggest that a reconsideration of Newman's understanding of the 'free act' of certitude, an act fulfilling our 'duty to be certain', challenges the assumptions of discussions like the above that the alternatives they propose are in fact exhaustive. As such it can contribute to a more informed appraisal of the problem of 'willing to believe' — a problem common to theology, philosophy of religion and philosophy.[27]

The second claim to be considered is Newman's claim that doubt is incompatible with the certitude which is essential to genuine religious commitment. It was generally concluded by

[24] 'Belief and Will', *Proc. Aristotelian Society Supplement* 28 (1954), p. 16.
[25] 'Belief and Will', *Religious Studies* 14 (Mar. 1978), p. 4.
[26] Ibid., p. 7.
[27] Cf. Bernard Williams, 'Deciding to Believe', *Problems of the Self* (Cambridge: At the University Press, 1973); Bernard Mayo, 'Belief and Constraint', *Proceedings of the Aristotelian Society* 64 (1963–4), reprinted in *Knowledge and Belief*, ed. A. Phillips Griffiths (Oxford: University Press, 1967).

Newman's contemporaries that the incompatibility of doubt which Newman defended necessarily implied that religious beliefs were rendered immune to criticism and that religious commitment was indefeasible (i.e. a 'come-what-may' commitment). Newman was charged with attempting to legitimate an uncritical dogmatism.

One British review of the *Grammar* protested that Newman's work only 'secures Certitude by isolating it from the processes of thought out of which it comes'.[28] An American review concluded that by the prohibition on doubt which Newman defended, the Roman Catholic church 'stifles thought; puts a premium on ignorance; is in open conflict with science; perpetuates its dogmas by making it sinful to call them in question'.[29] The same charge was reputedly directed against Roman Catholics in a less tactful form as well; W. G. Ward described one Victorian reaction which considered Catholics 'external to the pale of intellectual civilization'.[30] Because Catholicism was thought to cultivate the 'intellectual maxim' of wilful suppression of doubt in the face of counter-evidence, a Catholic was no more able to be argued with, they said, than was a 'savage'.

The challenge was to religious believers in general, as was clear in W. K. Clifford's passionate denunciation of dogmatism addressed to non-Catholics and Catholics alike. Assuming that beliefs that were founded on 'insufficient evidence' could only be maintained by wilful suppression of doubt, Clifford branded as sinners those who believe on such ground:

If a man, holding a belief which he was taught in childhood or persuaded of afterwards, keeps down and pushes away any doubts which arise about it in his mind, purposely avoids the readings of books and the company of men that call in question or discuss it, and regards as impious those questions which cannot easily be asked without disturbing it — the life of that man is one long sin against mankind.[31]

Because religious belief overstepped the boundaries of

---

[28] *The Edinburgh Review* 132 (Apr. 1870), pp. 411–12.

[29] *The Biblical Repertory and Princeton Review* 43 (Apr. 1871), p. 244.

[30] Ward II, p. 272.

[31] W. K. Clifford, 'The Ethics of Belief', originally published in *Contemporary Review* 29 (Jan. 1877); reprinted in *Lectures and Essays, Vol. II* (London: Macmillan, 1901), p. 175.

legitimate belief by making inferences concerning what is 'contrary to, or outside of, the uniformity of nature',[32] religious commitment was condemned.

The question that was thereby raised in Newman's time is, as we shall see later, still raised today — namely, is the claim that doubt is incompatible with faith only understandable in terms of wilful suppression of doubt and the obverse 'will to be certain'?[33] As with the first claim about the free act of will, I suggest that an analysis of Newman's claim about doubt can be valuable to contemporary philosophy of religion in several respects.

At a general level Newman's value to studies of the problem of religious commitment lies in his marked concern with analysing the *resistance* to change in belief that characterizes commitment. Theological accounts of faith often make reference to religious commitment in terms of resisting temptation to abandon belief, or in terms of an intention to maintain the commitment. It is surprising, therefore, that explicit theoretical analyses of religious commitment have neglected that aspect of resistance.[34] Even where intention and obligation are treated as parameters of commitment, the implications are not drawn out in terms of the admissions which are possible or necessary to the believer concerning the dubitability and corrigibility of his beliefs.[35] A study of Newman's detailed concern with the problem of intellectual tenacity and resistance to change in belief should, therefore, prove very fruitful.

At a more specific level, Newman can contribute in the following ways. First, he distinguishes between the doubt that is descriptively incompatible (i.e. is precluded) and the doubt that is prescriptively incompatible (i.e. should be

---

[32] Ibid., p. 204.   [33] E.g. William Bartley III; see Chap. IV.

[34] E.g. Robert Rex Dolan, 'An Analysis of Religious Commitment' (Ph.D. dissertation, Columbia University, 1955). Even Basil Mitchell's excellent book, *The Justification of Religious Belief* (New York: Seabury, 1973) does not deal with the question of the *precise* character of the refusal to abandon the belief, the inability to imagine oneself mistaken or the intention to remain commited.

[35] Cf. Margaret Farley, 'A Study in the Ethics of Commitment Within the Context of Theories of Human Love and Temporality' (Ph.D. dissertation, Yale University, 1973). Needless to say, drawing out such implications would have been foreign to the aims and approach of this dissertation.

consciously excluded). Secondly, Newman offers valuable suggestions concerning different senses of doubt, some of which he sees as incompatible with faith, some of which as not incompatible.

The implications of these contributions will be developed in the following ways. First, I intend to exhibit the warrant for suggesting that in Newman's work there is an important, but as yet inadequately appreciated, position on genuine religious adherence involving the claim that not all possible doubt is 'reasonable' in a given case, and that only 'reasonable' doubt precludes certainty. That warrant is both indirect (i.e. claims about the relation between prescription and description concerning 'right reasoning') and direct (i.e. claims about the 'dubitability' that is compatible with certitude). Much of what he says can, I think, be illuminated by reference to positions on 'reasonable doubt' in the twentieth century.

Secondly, I intend to consider a variety of prima-facie indications in Newman's work supporting a picture of uncriticizable religious commitment: namely the incompatibility of doubt, the indefectibility of certitude, intolerance of counter-evidence, and the 'promise' never to change. I suggest that a re-examination of these elements in Newman's thought can reveal the possibility of an alternative picture of religious commitment. A number of independent aspects of Newman's thought reinforce one another and converge toward the conclusion that Newman's prohibition on doubt is not meant to and does not entail ultimate immunity from criticism. Instead, his prescriptions against doubt (and his claims about the 'independence' of assent and certitude from inference) are meant to urge a particular *mode* of adherence, allowing criticizability but nevertheless in an important sense 'unconditional'. Affirmations of the corrigibility of religious certitudes and the possibility of warranted abandonment of religious commitment can be found in Newman's work. Religious commitment, at least according to this strand, is not unqualified; it does not involve the undertaking of an indefeasible obligation to maintain the commitment 'come what may'. And this co-exists with a strong emphasis on the 'personal' relationship involved in religious commitment.

Once again, the importance of a study of Newman's position (holding in tension, as it does, these contrasting emphases) should be evident.

This position on religious commitment and its relation to doubt to which I am pointing is not the only one to be found in Newman's work. However, these two aspects of this strand are tied to crucial parts of his thought in such a way as to make elaboration of it a necessary part of Newman exegesis. My task then is to assemble these reminders of a neglected side of Newman's thought. In addition, whether or not it is his 'definitive' position, it is the position which can be of most value to contemporary philosophy of religion, by suggesting ways to reconcile a commitment which is both rational and yet 'unconditional' in a significant sense.

My examination of Newman's thought will deal particularly, though not exclusively, with the *Essay in Aid of a Grammar of Assent* (1870) and the earlier papers on faith and certainty.[36] It should be noted that Newman's contributions to the problem of religious commitment are contoured by the admitted limits of even the mature formulation of his model of religious commitment. Newman wrote to Father Walford in 1870 about his *Grammar*:

As to my book, it is always most difficult to be exact in one's language, nor is it necessary to be exactissimus in a work which is a conversational essay, not a didactic treatise. It is like a military reconnaissance. . . . It is a preliminary opening of the ground.[37]

He did not see the *Grammar* as definitive; in a letter in 1871 Newman commented as follows:

I am sensible it may be full of defects, and certainly characterized by incompleteness and crudeness, but it is something to have started a problem, and mapped in part a country, if I have done nothing more.[38]

Newman's claim to the contrary notwithstanding, he does try to achieve clear and precise distinctions in the *Grammar*; however, that work (and *a fortiori* the papers preceding it) is often still only suggestive, its insights inadequately formu-

---

[36] *G.A.*; *The Theological Papers of John Henry Newman on Faith and Certainty* (*T.P.*). Henceforth all parenthetical references to page numbers, unless otherwise qualified, will be to the *Grammar*.

[37] Letter, 21 May 1870, cited by A. J. Boekraad, *The Personal Conquest of Truth According to John Henry Newman* (Louvain: Editions Nauwelaerts, 1955), pp. 170-1.   [38] Ward II, pp. 270-1.

lated. Newman's modest self-evaluation is no doubt justified in part, but it is also important to remember that the 'defects' and 'incompleteness' are at times understandable in the light of the intellectual limits of his historical context. Newman started with the contrasts and categories that were given by that context. That he was weighed down by certain inherited formulations does not of course excuse errors on his part. But it does justify a serious attempt on our part to avoid ignoring fundamentally correct insights by concentrating on exposing technical problems. What Newman said of himself in his *Essay on the Development of Christian Doctrine* seems appropriate to remember here: 'These sentences, whatever be the errors of their wording, surely express a great truth.'[39] There are errors in his thought on certitude and doubt and these will be pointed out. But it is also appropriate to do some reconstruction, where necessary, to reveal whatever 'great truths' may be there. Most importantly, one can learn something from Newman's formal philosophical programme of justifying certitude in concrete cases without having to accept as legitimate *all* his religious applications of the principle.

A second limitation inherent in the *Grammar* concerns the distinction between religious belief and *divine faith*. Although Newman makes the distinction in his works between a natural religious belief and a divine gift of grace, he disclaims any intention of treating divine faith as such in the *Grammar*. He sets out there to examine the assent which follows religious inquiry. His aim is to investigate 'what the mind does, when it contemplates, when it makes an act of faith', but he immediately qualifies this, saying it is 'not precisely faith, because faith, in its theological sense, includes a belief, not only in the thing believed, but also in the ground of believing' (99). That is, a treatment of divine faith in itself would involve treatment of belief in doctrines 'expressly because God has revealed them' (99–100); such treatment is beyond the scope of Newman's discussion in the *Grammar*.

However, although the analysis is restricted to the context of religious inquiry and religious belief, rather than the

---

[39] *Dev.*, p. 175.

divinely infused gift of faith, it is nevertheless concerned with the character of genuine religious commitment. The *Grammar* is for the most part devoted to a study of the certitude that is possible as a result of religious inquiry. Even if distinct from the certainty of divine faith, the certainty of religious belief is nevertheless constitutive of 'vital Christianity' and 'Christian earnestness' (238, 239):

... religion demands more than an assent to its truth; it requires a certitude, or at least an assent which is convertible into certitude on demand. Without certitude in religious faith there may be much decency of profession and of observance, but there can be no habit of prayer, no directness of devotion, no intercourse with the unseen, no generosity of self-sacrifice. (220)

It seems appropriate to conclude that an analysis of this certitude, and the doubt that is incompatible with it, will provide an understanding of what Newman requires for genuine religious commitment. (The relation of this commitment to divine faith will be considered at the very end of our inquiry.)

Chapters I and II will introduce the problem of the status of certitude in Newman's thought and elaborate his understanding of non-analytic reasoning. This provides an *indirect* approach to the question of the role of the will in certitude, and ultimately to the question of the relation of doubt to religious commitment. Chapter III examines in some detail the ambiguity concerning the 'control of the will' which Newman describes, and argues that Newman's understanding of the relation between willing and certitude involves two different roles of the will.

Chapters IV, V, and VI examine the kind of persistence and resistance to change in belief which Newman sees as part of religious commitment. The claims that assent is incompatible with doubt and that certitude is incompatible with doubt are analysed into suggestions concerning kinds of doubt that are compatible with each, and kinds that are not compatible. Moreover, the spontaneous passive adherence that is part of certitude is distinguished from the active deliberate adherence which is legitimated by certitude. Finally the question of the criticizability that is ruled out or implied by his understanding of doubt and commitment is addressed. Chapter VII deals with the relation of 'divine faith' to religious certitude.[40] It asks what constitutes the uniqueness of the gift of divine faith, and considers whether the earlier conclusions concerning dubitability and criticizability are relevant to the question of adherence to and abandonment of divine faith.

---

[40] It will be noted that I have used the terms 'certitude' and 'certainty' without distinguishing them. I do so because although Newman made a distinction he did not maintain it consistently and, as I shall later argue, its use in his thought needs to be reinterpreted.

CHAPTER

I

> My surmise is, that he [Rogers] thinks me a pro-
> foundly sceptical thinker, who, determined on not
> building on an abyss, have, by mere strength of will,
> bridged it over, and built upon my bridge — but that
> my bridge, like Mahomet's Coffin, is self-suspended,
> by action of the will.
>
> Letter from Newman to Mrs Froude
> 7 August 1865

A correct understanding of Newman's view of the relation between religious commitment and doubt depends on a correct understanding of his view of the role of the will in certitude. It is, more often than not, misunderstandings of the relation between willing and certitude which generate misunderstandings of Newman's prescriptions against doubting. In order to prepare the way for a more precise understanding of the role of the will in certitude and doubting, this chapter and the following one will *indirectly* address the problem by considering Newman's view of the limits and achievements of our human reasoning ability. It seems appropriate to begin with two brief introductory sections which will first locate the concept of 'certitude' in the larger context of Newman's thought on 'assent', and then raise the question of the status of 'certitude'.

1. Assent: Its Conditions and Varieties

Several times in the year 1860 Newman described his intentions concerning his proposed *Grammar*; basically it would be an attempt to show that a 'popular', 'practical' and 'personal' way of reasoning, as legitimate as the scientific or demonstrative way, could in religion (as in other subjects) justify an 'unconditional acceptance' of, or 'assent' to, a

proposition.[1] Newman prepared the way for his characteriza-
tion of assent in the *Grammar* by distinguishing it from two
other attitudes or relations he thought an agent could have
toward a proposition — namely, 'doubt' and 'inference'.

Although Newman admitted that the word 'doubt' could
be used to mean the 'deliberate recognition of a thesis as
being uncertain', he informed his readers that he would use it
in the *Grammar* to mean 'suspense of mind' (7). That is, to
have 'no doubt' about a proposition *p* is equivalent to either
inferring or assenting to *p* — 'when we infer, we do not doubt
... and when we doubt, we cannot assent' (5–6). Thus, to
doubt *p* is to withhold assent or inference from both *p* and
not-*p*. It is interesting to note that this definition of doubt
accords with a standard modern philosophical usage, where
'To be in doubt about a proposition is to withhold assent
both from it and from its contradictory.'[2] His use of the
term in the *Grammar* is clearly restricted to such suspense
of assent.[3] Although Newman thought he could 'dismiss' the
concept with a few words in the early pages of the *Grammar,*
we shall see that it retains a crucial importance for his whole
understanding of certitude and religious adherence as proposed
in the *Grammar*. In addition, this same understanding of
doubt as withholding assent is what is judged to be incompatible with faith in other of Newman's writings.[4]

Inference and assent differ from doubt in that they are
both *acceptances* of a proposition, but they differ radically
from each other with respect to the quality or character of
that acceptance. Assent is an 'unconditional', 'unqualified',
'absolute' acceptance of a proposition; inference is 'conditional'.

Before developing the concept of 'unconditionality' and
its opposite, Newman introduced the idea of 'apprehension'
(the 'imposition of a sense on the terms' of a proposition (9))

---

[1] Harper, pp. 131–2 (letter to Froude, 18 Jan. 1860) and *T.P.*, p. 82 (5 Jan. 1860).

[2] Cf. *Encyclopedia of Philosophy*, reprint ed. 1972, s.v. 'Doubt', by Harry G. Frankfurt, p. 412.

[3] In one early paper (13 May 1853) Newman defines 'doubt' as 'conditional assent' rather than suspense of mind, but he seems to have discarded that termin-ology later.

[4] *V.M. I*, p. 85, n. 4; p. 108, n. 2.

and elaborated its two modes — 'real' and 'notional'. Real apprehension is directed to images, units, the concrete; notional apprehension is directed to the general, the abstract. Both real and notional apprehension have one origin — 'sense and sensation' (34); what distinguishes them is the *mode* of apprehension of the object.[5]

Newman's general purpose seems to have been to point to the existence and importance of an apprehension which is affective, imaginative, and thus self-involving, but his descriptions of the differences between the two kinds of apprehension prompted significant criticisms by his contemporaries, as well as by modern writers.[6] More important, a number of Newman's contemporary and modern critics have objected to his view of the amount of apprehension necessary for assent.[7] Newman admitted that apprehension is a necessary condition of assent, but judged that apprehension of

[5] I take issue here with those understandings in which the distinction refers to the objective character of propositions rather than to the mode of appropriation. Jay Newman suggests that the distinction 'is based upon the nature of the terms in the proposition being apprehended' ('Cardinal Newman's Phenomenology of Religious Belief', *Religous Studies* 10 (June 1974), p. 130). James Collins argues that the difference is a function of the 'precise object under acceptance', either the proposition 'as such' or the existent being intended by the proposition (*Philosophical Readings in Cardinal Newman* (Chicago: Henry Regnery, 1961), p. 21).
    There are remarks in the *Grammar* which suggest this (e.g. pp. 22–3, 37), but since Newman admits that a proposition may admit of both kinds of apprehension at the same time (either by different individuals, p. 10, or in the same mind, p. 11) the apprehension, rather than the independent object, must possess the force.

[6] F. D. Maurice, 'Dr. Newman's *Grammar of Assent*', *The Contemporary Review* 14, May 1870; author of review article in *The Biblical Repertory and Princeton Review*, Apr. 1871 (pp. 238 ff). H. H. Price, *Belief*, Muirhead Library of Philosophy (London: George Allen & Unwin Ltd., 1969), pp. 330–4; also see pp. 316–30, 340–8 for an excellent discussion of the various possible meanings of 'image' and 'notion'. Consult Pailin, *The Way to Faith: An Examination of Newman's 'Grammar of Assent' as a Response to the Search for Certainty in Faith* (London: Epworth Press, 1969), Appendix I, pp. 198–200 for a good treatment of the ambiguity and/or confusion in Newman's classification of real and notional assents.

[7] Jay Newman, 'Cardinal Newman's Phenomenology of Religious Belief', and Martin D'Arcy, *The Nature of Belief* (London: Sheed & Ward, 1931) argue that Newman devalues notional assents. Jouett Powell argues, however, that there is no necessary primacy of real over notional in *all* of the contexts of discourse Newman used; see his *Three Uses of Christian Discourse in John Henry Newman: An Example of Non-Reductive Reflection on the Christian Faith*, Dissertation Series 10 (Missoula, Montana: Scholars' Press, 1975).

the predicate 'is true' is sufficient apprehension if we have reason to trust the authority which presents the proposition to us. Since Newman claimed that the '*Essay* [on Assent] begins with refuting the fallacies of those who say that we cannot believe what we cannot understand',[8] it is clear that difficulties with his view of apprehension constitute significant difficulties for at least the early part of the *Grammar*. Newman's objective for the second part of the book, however, need not depend on the success of the first aim. He intends to show that we can legitimately believe what we cannot prove; this need not require the particular view of apprehension Newman maintains in the first half. This conclusion is supported by C. S. Dessain's judgement that 'it is hardly an exaggeration to say that the *Grammar of Assent* is really two books'.[9] Therefore, it seems possible to ignore the problems with apprehension at this point; they will be more fittingly discussed when we later consider the implications of Newman's view of religious commitment to a Divine Person.

In focusing on the second objective of the *Grammar* we return to the distinction between 'conditional' and 'unconditional'. Newman's particular project was to show how a 'conditional acceptance of a proposition, − such as is an act of inference, − is able to lead as it does, to an unconditional acceptance of it, − such as is assent' (157). 'Conditionality' means two things for Newman. First, it means having *degrees* − assent is 'indivisible' while inference varies in strength (38).[10] Secondly, conditionality means *being dependent on*

---

[7] Fitzjames Stephen, 'On a Theory of Dr. Newman's as to Believing in Mysteries', paper for Metaphysical Society, 12 Jan. 1875 (cited in James C. Livingston, *The Ethics of Belief: An Essay on the Victorian Religious Conscience*, AAR Studies in Religion 9 (Missoula, Montana: Scholars' Press, 1974), p. 23).

Review article, 'Dr. Newman's *Grammar of Assent*', *Edinburgh Review* 132, 1870, p. 408. F. D. Maurice, 'Dr. Newman's *Grammar of Assent*', *The Contemporary Review* 14 (May 1870), p. 156. Also cf. Pailin, *The Way to Faith*, pp. 105–8.   [8] *G.A.*, p. 495, Note II.

[9] C. S. Dessain, 'Cardinal Newman on the Theory and Practice of Knowledge. The Purpose of the *Grammar of Assent*', *Downside Review* 75 (Jan. 1957), p. 3.

[10] R. A. Naulty suggests that the issue of indivisibility of assent is a pseudo-dispute between Newman and Locke; see 'Newman's Dispute with Locke', *Journal of the History of Philosophy* 11 (Oct. 1973), p. 453. (A number of Newman's contemporaries also felt the issue was terminological.)

premisses — assent is 'unqualified' adhesion because it is independent of its premisses in some sense. The precise nature of both this indivisibility and this independence will become clearer when we consider Newman's view of legitimate adherence and abandonment of beliefs (Chapters IV, V, and VI). For the moment it suffices to note that for Newman inference is a necessary condition of assent, but not an exhaustive explanation of it.

Most of our unconditional acceptances of propositions — our assents — are unconscious, given without a direct knowledge of what we are doing (189). Usually 'by degrees and without set purpose, by reflection and experience, we begin to confirm or to correct' them (194). In addition to the ordinary experience of our daily lives, however, explicit examinations can test our initial assents. These should be undertaken by educated persons as a matter of course (192), as well as whenever our assents are challenged. A 'conscious' and 'deliberate' assent (183) to our unconscious assent is termed a 'conviction', a 'reflex' or 'complex' assent.

Such complex assents, when objectively valid, are called 'certitudes' (196, 197, 221). We can for the moment bracket the question whether Newman maintains, or is correct in maintaining, that *only* objectively valid complex assents are genuine certitudes; Newman's final position on this can only be determined after a complete assessment of his views on certitude. For the moment, we can at least put certitude in the larger context of assent and inference as follows: certitude is a 'complex act' composed of both the simple and reflex assents and characterized by both 'repose and persistence' (216).

2. The 'Complex Act' of Certitude

Having located certitude as a variety of reflex assent, we can ask what is the status of this 'complex act'; how is certitude related to the will? In other words we can begin to address the following question: from what do the repose and persistence derive, and in what does the persistence consist?

In Newman's writings between the years 1853 and 1870 we find two kinds of description of certitude. On the one hand, we find certitude described in the *Grammar* as a 'perception of a truth with the perception that it is a truth, or the consciousness of knowing' (197). On the other hand, we find in an early paper (1865) in preparation for the *Grammar,* Newman's claim that 'certitude is not the compulsory effect of any process of argument as its proper cause . . . but a free act (to speak generally), just as the acts of conscience are free and depend upon our will'.[11] Newman elaborates this when he writes a few lines later that 'when it is a duty to be certain, one ⟨we⟩ must do one's ⟨our⟩ best to fulfill the duty'. We have already seen, moreover, that in the *Grammar* certitude is defined as a 'conscious' and 'deliberate' reflex assent. In addition, the process of reaching certitude is said there to be one in which the mind goes 'from merely probable antecedents to the sufficient proof of a fact or a truth, and, after the proof, to an act of certitude about it (329).

References to a 'free act' dependent 'upon the will', a 'conscious' and 'deliberate' act, 'after the proof', seem to conflict with the description of certitude as a knowledge or perception. They seem, in addition, to provide explicit support for what David Pailin has called a necessary implication of Newman's fundamental assumptions concerning inference and assent. Pailin has argued that given Newman's claim that inference can never logically entail assent, certitude can only be an act of will distinct from and following the reasoning process, a 'choice made by the individual'.[12] Since inference is always 'conditional' and assent is always 'unconditional', assent belongs to the 'logic of personal decision and not to that of reasoned conclusions'; however much 'apprehension, reasoning and conscience influence the decision to believe . . . the actual act of assent is a leap across a logical gulf which these factors can never bridge'.[13] Newman's answer to the problem of how to get from a conditional inference to an unconditional acceptance is thus said to lie in placing the two in different categories, namely the respective categories of 'reasoning' and 'commitment' (where commitment is allied to 'decision' or 'choice').

---

[11] *T.P.,* p. 121 (1865) arrow brackets in the following quotations indicate Newman's own interlinear additions.
[12] Pailin, *The Way to Faith,* p. 103.   [13] Ibid., p. 173; p. 175.

Pailin is not alone in seeing Newman's concept of 'certitude' as referring to the result of a decision bridging a logical gulf. Because of his claim that assent is a 'free act' for which we are responsible, Newman has recently been classified as a 'volitionalist' along 'Cartesian' or 'Kierkegaardian' lines.[14] In addition, the view that certitude is for Newman a choice or decision is subscribed to, although implicitly, by a number of other accounts which charge that after all is said and done Newman remains a sceptic.[15] If Newman did in fact admit that reason could not reach complete certitude, then only an act of will in the form of a decision could bridge that gap.

This interpretation of the 'free act of will' suggests a fruitful, though indirect, way of approaching Newman's texts on certainty and the will. This indirect way, which will be followed in the remainder of this chapter and the following one, consists in considering Newman's *general* response to the following questions: Can the distinction between inference and assent be understood only in terms of a 'logical gulf' bridged by a choice following reasoning; does the freedom or non-entailment of assent require that certitude be effected by a choice or decision to fill in a gap between reasoning's conclusions and complete assurance? In this and the following chapter I want to show more precisely than has yet been done the reasons why an affirmative answer to these questions is incorrect *either* as an understanding of Newman's overall position on certitude or as an understanding of a 'contradictory' element in his thought.[16]

3. The Analytic Paradigm and the Transcendentalist Solution

Newman's answer to the question whether the act of certitude need be interpreted as something distinct from and following the reasoning process is revealed in embryo in the

[14] Louis Pojman, 'Belief and Will', *Religious Studies* 14 (Mar. 1978).
[15] See Chap. II, Sect. 4.
[16] William Fey accepts without criticism the claim that certain passages in Newman's work clearly refer to a choice through which certitude is reached (*Faith and Doubt: The Unfolding of Newman's Thought on Certainty* (Shepherdstown, Va.: Patmos Press, 1976), p. 114). See also pp. 120, 122, 140, 142, 148 and *passim* 114–18 where a vacillation seems to be assumed.

following passage, the importance of which justifies quoting Newman's own words at length:

There are those, who, arguing *a priori*, maintain, that, since experience leads by syllogism only to probabilities, certitude is ever a mistake. There are others, who, while they deny this conclusion, grant the *a priori* principle assumed in the argument, and in consequence are obliged, in order to vindicate the certainty of our knowledge, to have recourse to the hypothesis of intuitions, intellectual forms, and the like, which belong to us by nature, and may be considered to elevate our experience into something more than it is in itself. (343-4)

Newman expresses his difference of opinion by continuing quite decisively: 'Earnestly maintaining, as I would, with this latter school of philosophers, the certainty of knowledge, I think it enough to appeal to the common voice of mankind in proof of it. That is to be accounted a normal operation of our nature, which men in general do actually instance' (344).

We can put together the following pieces of information concerning Newman's position. He agrees with the premiss — experience leads to probabilities — since it is qualified by the phrase 'by syllogism'.[17] He also agrees with the conclusion of the second group — we can reach certainty — but diverges sharply in his rejection of their recourse to intuition and other such principles. He refuses to accept the claim, implicit in such recourse, that our experience needs to be elevated 'into something more than it is in itself'. It is, Newman suggests, enough to appeal to the 'normal operation of our nature'.

The significance of this passage is that it is a prima-facie rejection of any explanation of our certainty which implies that our experience, our natural reasoning processes, *as* they *are*, cannot give us the certainty we desire and experience. In particular, I suggest that the rejection applies also to any claim that because the premisses do not logically entail the conclusion, we must bridge the gap by a choice. Indirect

---

[17] Meynell wrote to Newman (9 Dec. 1869) as follows: 'I am not to understand, am I? that you admit the antecedent of those who argue that because "experience only leads to probabilities, certitude is a mistake"?' Newman replied that he did accept the premiss because he had written 'experience *logically* only leads to probabilities' (10 Dec. 1869). Cited by Zeno, *John Henry Newman, Our Way to Certitude: An Introduction to Newman's Psychological Discovery: The Illative Sense and His 'Grammar of Assent'* (Leiden: E. J. Brill, 1957), pp. 265-6.

support for this extrapolation is suggested by a recent philosophical discussion which is strikingly similar to Newman's phrasing of the problem in this passage. A brief examination will highlight Newman's insight, by making more explicit one account of the reasons for rejecting both scepticism and those hypotheses which attempt to bridge a gap between our natural experience and total certainty.

The discussion I refer to is John Wisdom's Gifford Lectures, delivered in 1950. As these remain unpublished I turn to two accounts of them, one by Renford Bambrough and the other by Stephen Toulmin.[18] Wisdom was concerned with what Newman called concrete inference, i.e. non-demonstrative conclusions whose evidence is of a different logical type. Some examples are conclusions about the future, the past, and other minds. Where evidence and conclusions are of different types, the conclusion cannot be analytically entailed. All concrete judgements involve such a 'trans-type' inference. Wisdom describes three approaches to the question of the validity of such inference, namely, (a) reductionistic, (b) transcendentalist (or 'intuitionist'), and (c) sceptical. Bambrough illustrates Wisdom's position as follows:

The position may be represented by an analogy with weighing on a pair of scales. The sceptic rightly observes that the weight in the evidence scale never balances the weight in the conclusion scale, and wrongly concludes that the conclusion is unjustified. The reductionist sees that the conclusion is justified, and wrongly concludes that the evidence does balance the weight of the conclusion. The transcendentalist recognizes both that the conclusion is justified and that the evidence does not balance its weight. He therefore offers a *makeweight* — something that will secure the balance between what is in the evidence scale and what is in the conclusion scale.[19]

That is, the sceptic sees the difference in type, the lack of entailment, as precluding certainty in the conclusion. The reductionist (e.g. the phenomenalist), fearing both sceptical and transcendentalist maneuvers, identifies the evidence and conclusion, claiming that they are mutual statements of each other in different idioms. The transcendentalist

---

[18] Renford Bambrough, *Reason, Truth and God* (London: Methuen, 1969); Stephen Toulmin, *The Uses of Argument* (Cambridge: University Press, 1958).

[19] Bambrough, *Reason, Truth and God*, pp. 69–70.

... recognizes that what is ordinarily counted as the ultimate evidence does not entail the conclusion. Since he also recognizes that the conclusion is nevertheless justified he tries to supply something else — an insight, an intuition, a transcendental mode of argument — which, when added to what is ordinarily recognized to be the ultimate evidence, *will* entail the conclusion.[20]

Underlying the strategies of all three, however, is the same assumption — that 'the scales must be in logical balance before the conclusion can be said to be justified'.[21]

Toulmin agrees with and elaborates Wisdom's negative judgement about this assumption underlying these three ways of approaching non-analytic, or what he calls 'substantial' argument. Pointing out the problems with the reductionist and transcendentalist approaches, Toulmin argues that the only alternative is scepticism, *as long as* we persist in trying to 'redeem' substantial arguments. 'All three shifts', however, he claims, 'are equally ineffective and all are equally unnecessary — if only we are prepared to give up the analytic ideal.'[22] The motive behind all three moves is a misguided valuation of analytic criteria of reasoning.

Toulmin claims that in the development of epistemology

... pride of place has been given to arguments backed by entailments; wherever claims to knowledge have been seen to be based on evidence not entailing analytically the correctness of the claim, a 'logical gulf' has been felt to exist which the philosopher must find some way either of bridging or of conjuring away, and as a result a whole array of epistemological problems have grown up around scientific, ethical, aesthetic, and theological claims alike.[23]

The development of logic has been the result of an attempt to provide *universal* forms and criteria for rationality. Logic by its own intent limits its domain, since only when abstracted from content are such forms necessarily valid. Logic has thus 'idealized' itself at the cost of much relevance. The absence of entailment in substantial argument is therefore, according to Toulmin, not the result of a 'lamentable weakness' in the arguments, but a function of the 'nature of the problems with which they are designed to deal'.[24] If we persist in

[20] Ibid., p. 69.
[21] Ibid., p. 70. It should be noted that Bambrough disagrees with Wisdom's rejection of transcendentalism, claiming that religion loses something crucial in Wisdom's account. [22] Toulmin, *The Uses of Argument*, p. 233.
[23] Ibid., p. 9 [24] Ibid., p. 168.

espousing the analytic model as applicable in all cases, we will try to 'patch-up' substantial arguments. We can succeed in justifying them for practical purposes, but on an analytic paradigm 'there is no denying the canker at their hearts'.[25]

The recourse to hypotheses like intuition is a function of seeing a 'logical gulf' where there is merely a type-jump;

Certainly substantial arguments often involve type-transitions in the passage from data and backing to conclusions; all this means is that we must judge each field of substantial arguments by its own relevant standards. The fundamental error in epistemology is to treat this type-jump as a logical *gulf.*[26]

For Toulmin, the substantial jump can be seen as a 'change in "direction" ', or 'change of *posture*',[27] a development which can be effected without a transcendental gap-filler of any kind.

Wisdom and Toulmin reject a strictly logical model of reasoning as paradigmatic, the sole provider of rational validity and certainty; they therefore reject all transcendentalism as well as scepticism. The parallel rejection by Newman, which we noted at the outset of this section, of both scepticism and particular transcendentalist strategies suggests a similar rejection on Newman's part of the paradigm on the basis of which such strategies are thought to be necessary. Such a rejection seems to obviate the need for Newman to have recourse to *any* hypothesis of the same status as the ones he explicitly disavows. That is, the rejection of an analytic paradigm in Newman's case would mean that in disavowing those particular transcendentalist solutions he implicitly disavows any sort of gap-bridger. And that suggested rejection of an analytic paradigm is indeed found in Newman's work — both explicitly and implicitly.

4. The Victorian Parallel

In the Victorian parallel to the situation described above the sceptical alternative was represented in part by the Oriel Noetics, the Evidential School of Oxford. For Newman the encounter with this way of thinking was centred in the

---

[25] Ibid., p. 154.   [26] Ibid., p. 234.   [27] Ibid., p. 251.

person of Richard Whately.[28] It is a commonplace that according to Whately's *Elements of Logic* 'all Reasoning, on whatever subject, is one and the same process, which may be clearly exhibited in the form of Syllogisms'.[29] It should be noted, however, that Whately equated 'Reasoning' with 'Argumentation' and renounced the idea that logic can be taken as 'furnishing the sole instrument for the discovery of truth in all subjects'.[30] Newman might well have agreed that all 'Argumentation', which he equated with 'Explicit Reason',[31] was able to be put in the form of syllogism;[32] he strongly affirmed the value of logical inference. What Newman probably found more unacceptable in Whately's position was the claim that Reasoning (Explicit Reason or Argumentation) was 'the most appropriate intellectual occupation of MAN, as man'.[33] Newman's disagreement with Whately concerned the *status* thereby given to Explicit Reason, the canonization of a syllogistic paradigm.

While the Noetics were direct and explicit proponents of a syllogistic paradigm, there were indirect proponents whom Newman had to face as well — namely, those scientific and theological minds whose concept of certainty was informed by the seventeenth-century developments which culminated in Locke's *Essay Concerning Human Understanding*. As a result of religious controversy in the seventeenth century, and in response to the challenge of radical scepticism, scientists and theologians alike took refuge in 'constructive scepticism', the view that while absolute certainty was impossible, one could gain adequate certainty.[34] 'Absolute infallible certainty' was the prerogative of God alone, but two kinds of certainty were possible to human beings: first a

---

[28] *Apo.* pp. 20-7. Cf. Thomas Vargish, *Newman: The Contemplation of Mind* (Oxford: Clarendon Press, 1970) for a discussion of early rationalist and empiricist influences on Newman. See R. D. Middleton's *Newman at Oxford* (London: Oxford University Press, 1950) for a more detailed account.

[29] *Elements of Logic* (New York: William Jackson, 1832), p. 184.

[30] Ibid., p. 189; preface x.

[31] *U.S.*, XIII, esp. p. 259; also cf. *G.A.*, p. 287, n.1.

[32] For example, several pages in the *Grammar* are devoted to the value of logical inference, the 'great principle of order in our thinking', pp. 285-7.

[33] Whately, *Elements of Logic*, preface xi.

[34] Henry Van Leeuwen, *The Problem of Certainty in English Thought 1630-90* (The Hague: Martinus Nijhoff, 1963).

'conditionally infallible certainty', sufficient for 'human purposes', was obtainable through mathematical and logical demonstration; secondly, 'moral certainty', sufficient for 'practical purposes', was possible in other cases.[35] Locke's view was both a widening and a narrowing of this position,[36] but the general tenor of the Royal Society by Newman's time was that no more than practical certainty was possible in either science or religion.

Charles Meynell, on reading the *Grammar*, reminded Newman of a man he, Meynell, had once met who denied the existence of certitude; that man claimed that

'it was the very A.B.C. of scientific men that it is the greatest mistake to make up one's mind once and for all *upon any subject whatsoever religious or otherwise*'. He told me that if anything in the world was demonstrated it was the impossibility of perpetual motion, but that he was not prepared to say that even that was an absolute truth.[37]

Newman's *Grammar* was in fact addressed to one of those scientists, his friend, the free-thinker, William Froude.[38] In a letter written in 1859 to Newman, Froude expressed the intellectual climate against which Newman was objecting:

More strongly than I believe anything else I believe this — that no subject whatever [sic] — distinctly not in the region of the ordinary facts with which our daily experience is consonant — distinctly not in the domain of history or of politics, and yet again a fortiori, not in that of Theology, is my mind, (or as far as I can take the mind of any human being,) capable of arriving at an absolutely certain conclusion.[39]

Froude admitted that 'Any probability however faint, may in its place make it a duty to *act as if* [emphasis his] the conclusion to which it points were absolutely certain', but continued: 'even the highest attainable probability does not

[35] Ibid., pp. 22-3; 35-7. This was the position enunciated by Chillingworth in the *Religion of Protestants* (1638) and by Tillotson. Both these men are referred to by Newman — and the former in the *Grammar*, the latter in the *U.S.*

[36] Locke thought that the existence of God could be demonstrated — cf. *An Essay Concerning Human Understanding*, Vol. II, Bk. IV, Chaps. 3 and 10. He also thought that assent in cases of the highest probability was not free but rather was compelled (cf. Van Leeuwen, p. 135). However, he judged as 'probability' what they had called a kind of 'certainty'.

[37] Letter to Newman, 4 Nov. 1869 (cited by Zeno, *Our Way to Certitude*, p. 261).

[38] Harper, pp. 19-21, where he notes Newman's letter to Froude (2 Jan. 1860), p. 127 and Froude's letter to Newman (8 Oct. 1864), p. 180. Cf. also James Collins, *Philosophical Readings in Cardinal Newman*, pp. 39-40.

[39] Harper, pp. 119-20.

justify the mind in discarding the residuum of doubt'.[40] Doubts, therefore, 'deserve to be cherished as sacredly as beliefs'.[41] The only 'pattern of Faith' he could accept was 'the temper, which, while it realizes as carefully as possible the exact degree of doubtfulness which attaches to its conclusions, *acts* [emphasis his] nevertheless confidently on the best and wisest conclusion it can form'.[42]

Froude argued against Newman that the gap between evidence and absolute certitude was less in science than in religion, but he nevertheless found the 'fundamental principle of universal doubt' to which he adhered as necessary in science as in religion.[43] The same 'temper' which was required in religion — namely, acting as if certain — was appropriate to science.[44] This resort to practical certainty indirectly exalts an analytic paradigm of certainty; though Froude claimed that in 'practical science ... more than elsewhere the principles and results of reasonings are confronted with the test of direct experiment',[45] his perennial objection to Newman's way of looking at religious certitude seemed to be related more to the non-demonstrability of concrete beliefs than to the superiority of scientific verification over religious. In Froude's case at least the empirical or strictly scientific challenge to religion was ultimately founded on the assumption of an analytic paradigm leading to the principle of 'universal doubt'.

Both the direct and indirect espousal of such an analytic paradigm led numerous Victorians to give up the idea of total certainty in concrete cases.[46] By showing the limits of strictly logical reasoning and by exploring the reaches of informal reasoning Newman intended to show that neither the sceptical alternative, nor the alternative that bridged a gap between practical and total certainty, was necessary.

The Aristotelian syllogism is the full and technical expression of the analytic paradigm; demonstration is the perfection of that reasoning in which language gains 'a monopoly on

[40] Ibid., p. 120. [41] Ibid., p. 121. [42] Ibid., p. 122.
[43] Ibid., p. 123. [44] Ibid., p. 122. [45] Ibid., p. 118.
[46] Cf. A. O. J. Cockshut, *The Unbelievers: English Agnostic Thought* (London: Collins, 1964).

thought' (263).[47] In the *Grammar* Newman repeatedly argued that however valid the deductive relation between premisses and conclusion, however valid the entailment, 'logic . . . does not really prove' (271), since it is still subject to a dependence on its premisses:

inference . . . even if demonstrative . . . is still conditional; it establishes an incontrovertible conclusion on the condition of incontrovertible premisses (172).

Even if the premisses are evident or axiomatic, the conclusion is conditional because it 'assumes' the premisses in the sense of depending on them.

This conditionality is compounded, however, when we try to apply formal reasoning to concrete cases. First, the premisses in this case are 'assumed' not merely in the sense of having the conclusion depend on them, but also in the sense of being 'not proven'. Secondly, by its own intent logic is limited to what can be abstracted and symbolized; it cannot reach *specific* conclusions. Abstract can only lead to abstract; logic has 'too much simplicity and exactness' to deal with the concrete (284). 'In its very perfection lies its incompetency to settle particulars and details' (284). In its realm it may be perfect, but its realm is severely limited. The abstract conclusion, even if demonstrative, fails to capture or correspond exactly with the concrete situation. It succeeds only in being probable with respect to particular items:

the margin between the abstract conclusions of the science, and the concrete facts which we wish to ascertain, will be found to reduce the force of the inferential method from demonstration to the mere determination of the probable. Thus, whereas . . . Inference starts with conditions, as starting with premisses, here are two reasons why, when employed upon questions of fact, it can only conclude probabilities; first, because its premisses are assumed, not proved; and secondly, because its conclusions are abstract, and not concrete (268-9).

Formal reasoning, even in demonstration, is conditional because it depends on premisses (40, 259, 264). Applied to concrete cases, the conditionality is deepened, the achievements of formal reasoning more limited (293).

---

[47] Cf. *U.S.*, 'Implicit and Explicit Reason', esp. pp. 257-9 where Newman treats the distinction between formal and informal reasoning later elaborated in the *Grammar*. Sermons X–XIV in general are useful in this respect (esp. pp. 199-200; 208-18; 229-30).

Like Wisdom and Toulmin after him, Newman suggests that

it is natural, then, to ask the question . . . why logic is made an instrumental art sufficient for determining every sort of truth, while no one would dream of making any one formula, however generalized, a working rule at once for poetry, the art of medicine, and political warfare? (358).

What is needed to remedy some of the inadequacy of formal inference with respect to those matters in which our life mainly consists is reasoning 'more delicate, versatile, and elastic than verbal argumentation' (271). Although in mathematics it would be wrong for us to give an assent without a strict demonstration, although we are justified there in withholding our assent until such a demonstration is given, this is not the case in concrete reasoning. It is natural that in mathematics we only assent on demonstration; but 'by a like dictate we are not justified, in the case of concrete reasoning and especially of religious inquiry, in waiting till such logical demonstration is ours, but on the contrary are bound in conscience to seek truth and to look for certainty by modes of proof, which, when reduced to the shape of formal propositions, fail to satisfy the severe requisitions of science' (412).

II

> You make too little of a move in thought which from
> a mass of data extracts and assembles what builds up
> into the proof of something which, though it doesn't
> go beyond the data, gives us an apprehension of
> reality which before we lacked.
>
> John Wisdom, 'The Logic of God'

The rejection of an analytic paradigm was the thrust of Newman's programme in the *Grammar*. It departed from the intellectual climate of his time, and thus presaged significant philosophical shifts which were to occur after him. In this chapter I shall consider Newman's understanding of the achievements of informal reasoning, with a twofold aim. First I want to describe Newman's claims — my argument that Newman did not have recourse to a gap-bridger (like deliberate volition) is supported as long as, according to Newman, the need for it is obviated. Secondly, I want to analyse his understanding in light of some contemporary philosophical suggestions on the topic of informal reasoning.

1. Implicit Reasoning

The mode of proof necessary in concrete matters lies in informal reasoning, reasoning which is 'more or less implicit, and without the direct and full advertence of the mind exercising it' (292). Such reasoning cannot be articulated — the reasons are too 'minute', 'abundant' and 'delicate' (291). 'Genuine proof' (271) in concrete matters is reached by a 'cumulation of probabilities, independent of each other' (288), converging and reinforcing each other, until one finally receives the conclusion without hesitation.[1] Newman

---

[1] Cf. Antony Flew's implication that this is an illegitimate 'ten-leaky-buckets' tactic (*God and Philosophy* (New York: Delta Bks., Dell Publ., 1966)) and Basil

describes the process as follows:

First he determines that the questions are such as he personally, with such talents or attainments as he has, may fairly entertain; and then he goes on, after deliberation, to form a definite judgement upon them; and determines them, one way or another, in their bearing on the bald syllogism which was originally offered to his acceptance. (291)

The 'bald syllogism' is the evidence considered as *strictly* logical proof; as such it is clearly inadequate. 'Taken in the letter' (293) these arguments are but probabilities. But they do not remain in the letter; they are evaluated and assessed by 'the action of our own minds, by our own individual perception of the truth in question, under a sense of duty to those conclusions and with an intellectual conscientiousness' (318). By considering the bearing of various questions on the 'bald syllogism', a person can come to

the conclusion, that he ought to accept it as true in his case . . . that this is a conclusion of which he can be certain, and ought to be certain, and that he will be incurring grave responsibility, if he does not accept it as certain, and act upon the certainty of it. (291)

This action of our minds is the use of the 'illative sense'. Newman uses this term, admittedly 'a grand name for a common thing',[2] to refer to the power of reasoning in general, covering the beginning, course and end of inquiry; it is the power of 'judging and concluding' (253). Sometimes the term covers this power both in its 'biassed and degraded' form as well as at the pitch of genius (331); at other times Newman uses it to refer to reasoning in its perfection (353).[3]

Though it does not provide a logical proof, such informal reasoning can lead to 'genuine' proof (271)[4] — i.e. genuine certainty. As a result of converging probabilities, the 'practised and experienced mind is able to make a sure divination that a conclusion is inevitable, of which his lines of reasoning do not actually put him in possession' (321).

One of Newman's contemporary critics, Leslie Stephen,

Mitchell's response (*The Justification of Religious Belief* (New York: Seabury Press, 1973), p. 40).

[2] Letter to Meynell, 17 Nov. 1869 (cited by Zeno, p. 263).

[3] Illative is also referred to as 'phronesis' (*G.A.*, pp. 354, 356; Ward pp. 248-9) and 'prudence' (*G.A.*, p. 317; *T.P.*, p. 24).

[4] Harper, p. 202 (29 Apr. 1879).

actually defends this understanding of proof in concrete cases. Recall Newman's description of the mathematical method of proof symbolized by the polygon inscribed in a circle: the conclusion in a concrete case is 'foreseen in the number and direction of accumulated premisses, which all converge to it, and as the result of their combination, approach it more nearly than any assignable difference, yet do not touch it logically (though only not touching it)' (321). Stephen agrees that in particular cases of concrete belief (such as Newman's examples of the mortality of men, and that Great Britain is an island) proof *is* generated by such an approximation method as Newman describes. These propositions are proven. Given a belief in the validity of induction, Stephen claims,

the proof of a matter of fact may approximate indefinitely to demonstration. It never actually reaches it, as the asymptote never actually reaches the curve. But the approximation is so close that human faculties will not enable us to distinguish the difference. The proof, that is, that two and two make four differs from the proof that men are mortal by so infinitesimal an amount as to be indistinguishable to the most sensitive mental vision.[5]

Stephen admits that a 'slight correction may be necessary to Locke's statement to justify our neglect of these infinitesimal quantities' but nevertheless argues that the 'validity' of Locke's ethic of belief is 'not sensibly affected'. Stephen's conclusion is that in such cases of concrete proof we are not disobeying Locke's maxim — we are not 'allowing belief to be more than the proofs will warrant'.[6]

Newman would no doubt have seen this (and rightly so) as support for his claims and a Pyrrhic victory for Locke. It was precisely this 'surplusage' of 'belief over proof' that Newman saw as the locus of his difference with Locke (300). Stephen's objection was not to Newman's *formal* claim about the possibility of proof in concrete cases but rather to the particular applications of it to which Newman extrapolated. Stephen agreed with Newman that the matter in some concrete cases can become 'as good as proved', 'as if it were

[5] 'Newman's Theory of Belief', *An Agnostic's Apology* (New York: G. P. Putnam's Sons, 1893), p. 221.

[6] Ibid., p. 222.

proved', 'amounting to a proof' (321).[7] Although the evidence
is not sufficient for a logical proof (i.e. although we cannot
'see' its cogency) we can 'feel' it;[8] we decide, says Newman,
'not that the conclusion must be, but that it cannot be otherwise. We say, that we do not see our way to doubt it, that it
is impossible to doubt, that we are bound to believe it, that
we should be idiots, if we did not believe' (317). Though it is
not logically demonstrated, a 'man would be irrational who
did not take it to be virtually proved' (323). The judgement
that it cannot be otherwise or that it is impossible to doubt
it is a judgement of complete certainty. There is no reservation, no room for doubt. Except in logical cases, a proof is
simply the 'limit of converging probabilities' (321), the result
of abundant contributions to a non-linear and unanalysable
process. In this way Newman foreshadowed the modern
rejection noted earlier of an analytic paradigm of certainty.

Newman thought it necessary to emphasize that the mind
is 'unequal to a complete analysis of the motives which carry
it on to a particular conclusion, and is swayed and determined by a body of proof, which it recognizes only as a
body, and not in its constituent parts' (292).[9] This emphasis
was required precisely because in his day he saw the *'onus
probandi'* thrown on the individual in a new way: 'now it
seems tacitly to be considered that a man ⟨he⟩ has no liberty
to believe, till it has been brought home to him in a rational
form that ⟨till he can state ⟨show cause⟩ distinctly, or at least
till others can do it for him, why⟩ he has a right to do so'.[10]
For Newman, 'the processes of reasoning which legitimately
lead to assent, to action, to certitude, are in fact too multiform, subtle, omnigenous, too implicit, to allow of being
measured by rule' (303). The conclusion is reached 'not by
any possible verbal enumeration of all the considerations'

---

[7] Hume contests Locke's division of all arguments into demonstrative and
probable — instead, he suggests 'we ought to divide arguments into *demonstra-
tions, proofs,* and *probabilities.* By proofs meaning such arguments from experience as leave no room for doubt or opposition.' See his *An Enquiry Concerning
Human Understanding,* Section VI, ed. Eric Steinberg (Indianapolis: Hackett
Publishing Company, 1977), p. 37, n. 24.

[8] *T.P.,* p. 17 (16 Dec. 1853).

[9] Cf. *U.S.,* X: pp. 199–200; XI: 208, 218; XIII: 267, 271; XV: 324.

[10] *T.P.,* p. 84 (12 Jan. 1860).

which effectively bring him to it, but 'by a mental compre-
hension of the whole case, and a discernment of its upshot'
(291).

Newman's conclusion that 'individuals need not be able to
analyse, understand, and explain their own grounds'[11] is
echoed by some modern philosophers. G. E. Moore put forth
the same claim in the first part of the twentieth-century:
there are many things we 'know' yet for which we cannot
give our reasons, hence we must *have* reasons which we cannot analyse.[12] Gilbert Harman offers a similar suggestion in
our decade, claiming that to assume that the reasons for
which people believe and which give them 'knowledge' are
conscious reasons is a mistake:

> The reasons for which people believe things are rarely conscious.
> People often believe things for good reasons, which give them
> knowledge, without being able to say what those reasons are. . . . It is
> doubtful that anyone has ever fully specified an actual piece of
> inductive reasoning, since it is unlikely that anyone could specify the
> relevant total evidence in any actual case. . . . One cannot always be
> sure what has influenced one's conclusion.[13]

George Mavrodes[14] and Alan R. White[15] agree with this
suggestion. Michael Polanyi also supports such implicit
reasoning, terming it 'subsidiary' as opposed to 'focal' knowing.[16] Such reasoning is not a lamentable makeshift which we
use but would avoid if we could; except in logical demonstration a proof is simply the 'limit of converging probabilities'
(321), and this is due to the 'nature of the case, and from the
constitution of the human mind' (293). As we noted in
Chapter I, John Wisdom's thought resembles Newman's in
significant ways. Wisdom claims that if we see nondemonstra-
tive reasoning as 'poor relations' (presumably the sort one
hides in shame), we 'make too little of a move in thought

---

[11] *T.P.*, p. 90 (27 Mar. 1860).
[12] 'A Defence of Common Sense' and 'Proof of an External World' in *Philosophical Papers* (London: Allen & Unwin Ltd., 1959).
[13] *Thought* (Princeton: Princeton University Press, 1973), pp. 28-9.
[14] *Belief in God*, Studies in Philosophy (New York: Random House, 1970),
pp. 12-13.
[15] 'On Claiming to Know', *Philosophical Review* 66 (1957), reprinted in
Knowledge and Belief, ed. A. Phillips Griffiths.
[16] *Personal Knowledge* (Chicago: University of Chicago Press, 1962), pp. 55-
65, 103.

which from a mass of data extracts and assembles what builds up into the proof of something which, though it does not go beyond the data, gives us an apprehension of reality which before we lacked'.[17] The only proof possible in concrete cases is an unanalysable complex of implicit, delicate and abundant non-logical contributions, and Newman realized long before others did that to deny that complex the status of proof is to reveal an implicit acceptance of an analytic paradigm of reasoning.

2. Natural Inference

Reference to the inability to analyse our reasons raises a number of interesting questions about the extent and implications of that inability; I shall approach these questions by examining Newman's view of 'natural inference'.

Newman's chapter on 'inference' is divided into three sections: 'formal inference', 'informal inference' and 'natural inference'. This might lead one to assume that natural inference was a third kind of inference, on the same level with formal and informal. In fact Newman seems to see this section as merely a continuation of the section on informal inference. His description, however, is ambiguous; it points to the possibility of a difference in degree between natural and informal inference, and may even point to the possibility of a difference in kind. This latter difference could have significant implications for a theory of justified belief.

Newman claims that informal inference is 'more or less implicit, and without the direct and full advertence of the mind exercising it' (292). Here he is referring to our inability to analyse adequately our reasons for our conclusions. He also says that in informal inference 'we grasp the full tale of premisses and the conclusion — *per modum unius,* — by a sort of instinctive perception of the legitimate conclusion in and through the premisses, not by a formal juxtaposition of pro-

[17] 'The Logic of God', in *Paradox and Discovery* (Berkeley: University of California Press, 1970), p. 13. Also see 'Gods', reprinted in *Religious Language and the Problem of Religious Knowledge,* ed. Ronald Santoni (Bloomington: Indiana University Press, 1968); *Other Minds* (Oxford, 1952); *Philosophy and Psycho-Analysis* (Oxford, 1953).

positions' (301-2). This description highlights the lack of conscious mediation involved.

The implication of the claim that informal reasoning is 'more or less implicit' — namely, that there are differences in degree of implicitness — seems to be borne out in the section on 'natural inference' where Newman describes a kind of reasoning that is '*altogether* unconscious and implicit' (330, emphasis mine). This suggests that natural inference may be the most immediate form of informal inference — differing in degree of conscious mediation.

Newman's claim, however, that in natural inference we 'pass promptly from one set of facts to another, not only, I say, without conscious media, but without conscious antecedents' (333) suggests the further possibility of a *qualitative* difference between kinds of informal inference. Newman seems to be distinguishing a case where inference has unconscious media from a case where it has both unconscious media *and* unconscious antecedents. It seems that inference might be considered informal as long as the mediation process is unconscious — and there might be degrees of that — but some inference (natural inference) might be immediate in a different way because *even* the antecedents are not recognized as such. Newman did not make much of this characteristic of unconscious antecedents; his failure to address himself to the possible distinction between informal and natural inference makes it difficult to determine his position.

Newman further describes this natural form of reasoning as one in which we go 'not from propositions to propositions, but from things to things, from concrete to concrete, from wholes to wholes. . . . Not only is the inference with its process ignored, but the antecedents also (330-1). This raises a second question. The claim that the antecedents are *ignored* implies that Newman saw natural inference as a totally unconscious version of a process which can be, and often is, conscious.[18] But the claim that we do not go from propositions

[18] C. S. Peirce is an example of someone who would see the antecedents as not merely 'ignored', but unable to be isolated or reconstructed. See, for example, 'A Neglected Argument for the Reality of God', *Charles S. Peirce: Selected Writings,* ed. Philip Wiener (New York: Dover Publ., 1958), pp. 359-68.

to propositions but from wholes to wholes might suggest, to those familiar with Wittgensteinian thought, the possibility of a way of reaching conclusions which is not an unconscious or covert inference. The question then is whether Newman's natural inference — an inference totally unconscious, even with respect to antecedents — is really an 'inference' at all.

There is one significant passage in Newman's papers on faith and certainty to which one can point for some support for the claim that he did not see it as inference at all; its detail and suggestiveness warrant quoting at length. In this 1860 paper Newman sketched a chapter of a book; it would cover the following points:

On reasoning as a simple progression or movement of the mind ... of which logic is only the nearest account, instead of being an analysis. On calculating boys, not *really* reasoning by *methods,* but by instinct. This will not easily be granted me. I was reading some one the other day, who said, *of course* the boys *did* go by method, though they could not bring it out — but I do not think it matters for my purpose, whether we say that the logic is implicit, or that there is no *real* logic except as symbolical.'[19]

That is, Newman allows that we could as easily say that there was no real logic involved as that the logic is implicit, that the boys did not go by method at all. In this way logic is only 'the nearest account' rather than an 'analysis'. Such a passage suggests that Newman could have been sympathetic to those who question whether all concluding is really an unconscious process isomorphic with conscious inference and *for that reason* justifying our conclusions. Such an interpretation of natural inference would also provide one way of understanding Newman's atypical claim that inference is 'ordinarily' the antecedent of assent (157).

On the other hand, however, we have Newman's clear affirmation that inference is a *sine qua non* condition of assent (41). If there must be an inference, then this 'unconscious' inference is really covert inference, merely an unconscious variety of a process of which all the steps are there but of which steps we are simply unaware. Moreover, Newman's claim that informal inference is really 'one and the same' with the logical form of inference (292) might be

[19] *T.P.*, p. 90 (27 Mar. 1860).

thought to apply to natural inference as well. Finally, his frequent references to the distinction between *having* reasons and *giving* reasons suggests that he saw the necessity of some kind of justifying inference. Most of the evidence, therefore, seems to support the view that Newman required at least a covert inference to justify assents. The position that inference of some kind is necessary to justify assents was common in Newman's day, and is not uncommon even today. Gilbert Harman, as we suggested earlier, seems to hold a position similar to that held earlier by G. E. Moore: knowing requires inference, so if it is not conscious inference it must be unconscious.[20] Newman's few interesting hints to the contrary may reveal the germ of a deeper insight into the way we reach conclusions — a way elaborated by Wittgenstein and his followers[21] — but an insight which he could not develop because of his commitment to a prevailing view of 'justified' belief.

Another question arises with respect to the status of the reasoning Newman is describing — the question is whether informal or natural inference is really *induction*. A number of Newman's contemporary critics charged Newman with ignoring the work on induction done by Mill and others, and therefore resorting to an unusual illative sense.[22] The difficulty in deciding the question is compounded by (1) the difficulty in determining the necessary and sufficient characteristics of an inductive argument, and (2) the difficulty in determining Mill's precise stand.[23] Moreover, on occasion Newman refers to the reasoning he discusses as 'induction',[24] but at other times opposes his view to that of Mill.[25] The question is too complicated to be resolved here. Suffice it to say at this point that if by induction is meant a non-demon-

---

[20] Cf. Harman, *Thought*, pp. 20–1; also see above notes nums. 32–5, preceding chapter.

[21] See works by Wittengenstein, Quine, and W. Sellars.

[22] Cf. Fitzjames Stephen, 'On Certitude in Religious Assent', *Frazer's Magazine* 5 (Jan. 1872), pp. 33–6; Leslie Stephen, 'Newman's Theory of Belief', *An Agnostic's Apology*, p. 222.

[23] For example, see Stephen Barker's 'Must Every Inference Be Either Deductive or Inductive?' *Philosophy in America*, Muirhead Library of Philosophy, ed. Max Black (Ithaca: Cornell University Press, 1965).

[24] *T.P.*, p. 19 (16 Dec. 1853).

[25] Ibid., pp. 19–20; see also *T.P.*, pp. 39–47 (4 May 1857).

strative *generalization*, Newman is not dealing with induction; if, on the other hand, it is admitted that problematic generalizations do not exhaust the category of inductive inferences, one can conclude that Newman contributed to the exploration of other conceptions of induction.

3. Change of Posture versus Logical Gulf

In contrasting formal and informal reasoning, Newman was adamant in his claim that informal reasoning is still conditional. The conclusion of an informal inference is dependent on premises which are not proven. In addition there is a lack of entailment — in concrete reasoning we add to the 'obscurity of the problem; for a syllogism is at least a demonstration, when the premises are granted, but a cumulation of probabilities . . . will vary both in their number and their separate estimated value, according to the particular intellect which is employed upon it' (293). The conclusion of the 'bald syllogism' is even more conditional than in formal inference; how then can it be unconditionally accepted? What else is needed to transform the inferential conclusion?

Newman thought his own answer to that question was given by his discussion of informal inference. He concluded the chapter by excusing his long and detailed treatment of informal inference, saying it was 'incumbent on me to illustrate the intellectual process by which we pass from conditional inference to unconditional assent' (329). Asking himself later, 'is there any *criterion* of the accuracy of an inference, such as may be our warrant that certitude is rightly elicited in favour of the proposition inferred, since our warrant cannot . . . be scientific?' Newman responded:

I have already said that the sole and final judgement on the validity of an inference in concrete matter is committed to the personal action of the ratiocinative faculty, the perfection or virtue of which I have called the Illative Sense . . . and I own I do not see any way to go farther than this in answer to the question (345).

The process of illation, *personal* reasoning, is the only answer.[26] The personal evaluation of the bearing of numerous

[26] The illative sense has been most conspicuously misunderstood by Martin D'Arcy, *The Nature of Belief* (London: Sheed & Ward, 1931), pp. 147-8.

considerations on the 'bald syllogism' presented to us is the sole and final judgement; it is effectively the unconditional acceptance.

The unconditional acceptance is not something that follows a personal evaluation; it is not the result of a choice. In his paper of 13 May 1853, Newman had written:

> The objective fact then which, viewed as a subject of conviction, is relative to premises, . . . or what is called evidence, when viewed as a subject of certainty, stands absolute and as a first principle and a starting point, as if with an axiomatic force; thus changed indeed in the order of viewing it ⟨its aspect⟩, but the same in this, that it is simply perceived by the mind.[27]

This change in 'the order of viewing' is what Toulmin calls a 'change of posture'.[28] Inference and assent, though different in the 'order of viewing', i.e., the viewed relation to premises, nevertheless are the same in that they are both 'simply perceived by the mind'. This implies that assent is no more the result of choice than is inference. The personal character of the reasoning is sufficient to account for the change in the 'order of viewing'. The informal inference *in itself* — i.e. simply considered in terms of the unproven premises and lack of entailment — is conditional, deserving only to be accepted with reservation. But Newman notes that 'the same set of considerations, which viewed abstractly [i.e. as strictly logical proof], may seem quite insufficient for certainty, may be conclusive when actually embodied or before the individual mind'.[29] A personal appraisal of the 'bald syllogism' can result in acceptance without reservation; we appropriate the conclusion unconditionally through a process of personal evaluation.

The illative judgement is clearly a personal one,[30] but no other test of our inference is possible (359) or necessary, according to Newman. Many of the contemporary criticisms of Newman centred on the charge that such a 'personal' sanction was inadequate; without a common standard, without a clear-cut set of criteria for truth, there remained only subjective psychological responses. We shall consider in detail

---

[27] *T.P.*, pp. 14–15 (13 May 1853). Arrow brackets indicate Newman's own addition.
[28] See Chap. I, Sect.3.   [29] *T.P.*, p. 88 (26 Jan. 1860).
[30] *G.A.*, pp. 302, 303, 317, 318; cf. also *T.P.*, p. 124 (20 July 1865).

in the following chapters the way in which Newman saw the relation between psychological description and epistemological norms. Here it is enough to add the reminder that Newman required that we reason with 'intellectual conscientiousness' (318), and with a concern for moral *and* intellectual character (302). In this way we can hope to arrive at the truth; people make mistakes, Newman admitted, but that only shows that we must be prudent, not that only demonstrative reasoning results in legitimate certitudes.

Newman's insight into the epistemological validity of personal reasoning is elaborated by a number of contemporary philosophers. Keith Lehrer, for example, considers the personal element extremely important in the justification of beliefs.[31] What justifies a man in believing *p* is the combination of the man's condition as an 'impartial and disinterested truth-seeker', and a certain kind of coherence of *p* with the rest of his belief system.[32] This 'veracious' man parallels Newman's intellectual and morally upright investigator.[33] Both Lehrer and Newman are joined by H. H. Price in seeing the personal element as having epistemic and not merely psychological value.[34]

Gilbert Harman likewise notes the importance of the personal contribution of the truth-seeker:

the test of good inference is not whether it corresponds with rules that have been discovered *a priori*. The test can only be whether the inference seems right to someone who does his best to exclude things that can lead him astray.[35]

Even in the case of what have been traditionally considered deductive rules of inference, Harman suggests we must revise our understanding. These rules, e.g. *modus ponens* (From *P* and If *P* then Q, infer Q), do not give us absolute rules for what we can accept:

there is no plausible rule of acceptance saying that if we believe both *P* and *If P then Q*, we may always infer or accept Q. Perhaps we should stop believing *P* or *If P, then Q* rather than believe Q.[36]

Individual assessments of *P* and *If P then Q* are necessary; there is no impersonally compelling rule which will relieve us of intellectual responsibility. What logic provides are the

---

[31] *Knowledge* (Oxford: Clarendon Press, 1974).   [32] Ibid., p. 212.
[33] *G.A.*, p. 311; also *U.S.*, XII.   [34] *Belief,* Lecture 10, pp. 471-3.
[35] *Thought,* pp. 18-19.   [36] Ibid., p. 157.

relations that obtain between propositions; this will not, however, tell us what to accept nor will it provide an invariable legitimation. Toulmin's observation that 'in logic as in morals, the real problem of rational assessment — telling sound arguments from untrustworthy ones . . . — requires experience, insight and judgement'[37] applies here as well.[38]

The element of the personal that is always present in any non-demonstrative proof is also indirectly pointed to by W. V. Quine and J. S. Ullian in their discussion of the criteria of justified belief.[39] Requirements of conservatism, generality, simplicity, refutability, and precision need to be applied to particular cases.[40] One of those judgements which Newman treats in some detail is that of conservative coherence — how well and easily does the belief in question fit in with the rest of the web of beliefs we operate with. In his comment that 'we see a proposition to be true, when we can make it dovetail closely into our existing knowledge, and when nothing else but it will so dovetail'[41] (i.e. will fit *that* closely), Newman foreshadowed Harman's conclusion that 'justification is not a matter of derivation from basic principles but is rather a matter of showing that a view fits in well with other things we believe'.[42] We seek the most explanation with the least change in our already existing belief system. This idea of 'maximum epistemic utility' is suggested by Newman when he says that our test of the truth of our conclusion, at least in part, is that 'when the conclusion is assumed as an hypothesis, it throws light upon a multitude of collateral facts, accounting for them, and uniting them together in one whole' (323). One of the marks of the sure divination of the conclusion which was 'as good as proved' is that of 'difficulties gradually clearing up' and 'unlooked-for correlations with received truths' (321). Such consistency, Newman realized, was not the 'guarantee' of truth, but there may, nevertheless, 'be a consistency in a

---

[37] Toulmin, *The Uses of Argument,* p. 188.

[38] Cf. Judith Jarvis Thomson, 'Reasons and Reasoning', *Philosophy in America,* ed. Max Black, p. 291.

[39] *The Web of Belief* (New York: Random House, 1970).

[40] Ibid., pp. 43–50, 65.   [41] *T.P.,* pp. 18–19 (16 Dec. 1853).

[42] *Thought,* p. 164; Newman would argue that it must not only fit in 'well', but must fit in *better* than anything else.

theory so variously tried and examplified as to lead to belief in it, as reasonably as' is the case in a 'court of law' (323).[43]

Our discussion of the personal nature of reasoning in concrete cases brings us back to Newman's claims concerning 'proof'. In concrete cases the matter can become 'as good as proved'. There is always 'in concrete matters incompleteness in the evidence of a fact',[44] but 'dimness in the evidence' and 'incomplete *notices* of truth' do not prevent genuine certainty, though they prevent logical proof.[45] If there is no logical proof, however, we need to ask whether Newman's claim to certainty was meant to refer to *practical* certainty.

4. Practical Certitude

Newman's claims have been interpreted both by Victorians and by modern commentators as implying scepticism and therefore as referring to *practical* certainty.[46] Leslie Stephen, in the decade following the publication of the *Grammar,* voiced from the non-believer's side the charge that Newman's view of reasoning implied scepticism.[47] Even earlier, Newman's views had been objected to by Catholic theologians, who assumed he was denying that *speculative* certainty was possible.[48] A number of modern accounts also claim that Newman's position implies scepticism or that the certainty he justifies is only the practical certainty sufficient for basing ethically good action on.[49]

[43] Ian Hacking, in *The Emergence of Probability* (Cambridge: University Press, 1975), discusses the close connection historically between legal reasoning and a concept of probability, pp. 85-91. Van Leeuwen, *The Problem of Certainty,* claims that the legal use of the idea of reasonable doubt owes much to Wilkins' development of that concept for theological reasons, p. 64.

[44] *V.M. I*, p. 88, n. 3.   [45] Ibid., p. 87, n. 9; p. 88, n. 6.

[46] Cf. Owen Chadwick, *The Mind of the Oxford Movement* (Stanford: Stanford University Press, 1960), pp. 42-4 for some of the grounds in Newman for the charge of scepticism.

[47] 'An Agnostic's Apology', p. 12 and 'Newman's Theory of Belief', pp. 238-40, in *An Agnostic's Apology* (these essays were originally published in the 1870s).   [48] *L.D.,* 11:289 (8 Dec. 1846).

[49] Cf. David Pailin, *The Way to Faith,* p. 167. J. M. Cameron's position is ambiguous. On the one hand he says that he wants to 'bring out (as against those who have argued ... that Newman was temperamentally and intellectually a sceptic who used the sceptical arguments to press men into faith) that Newman at certain points deepened the empiricist position to show that the logical issues were more complex than Hume, for example, had supposed, and that here the

In a letter to Newman in 1869 his friend Meynell wrote: 'When you speak of Certitude, . I think of apodictical certitude, whereas yours is the practical certitude.'[50] Meynell concluded that because they were in two 'different grooves' — Meynell being more interested in abstract questions, and Newman in their concrete applications — Newman must be referring to practical certainty. Newman did not directly respond to this question, but his whole programme clearly rejected such practical certitude as the highest achievement possible.

Practical certitude refers to the adequacy of the evidence for purposes of acting in given ways; it consists in an assurance sufficient for acting on the belief, but not sufficient for an unhesitating judgement that the belief is certain. The warrant for practical certitude can be either theoretical or practical. On the one hand, the warrant can be arguments or theoretical evidence which is not perfect but is sufficient to justify acting on the basis of the belief. On the other hand, practical certitude can have a practical source. One such source is the *need* for a given action which presupposes the particular belief. Kant's absolute need for moral behaviour, for example, legitimates acting as if God exists (i.e. gives certainty sufficient for acting in that way) without necessarily legitimating a declaration without doubt that God exists.[51]

Whatever the source of practical certitude, it remained for Newman an 'opinion which it is safe and wise to take as true', but not more than that.[52] In many cases practical certitude is all we can get, but that is due to the peculiarities of the particular case and is not a general function of the non-demonstrability of a proposition:

strongest currents in his thought make against scepticism' ('Newman and Empiricism', *The Night Battle* (London: Catholic Book Club, 1962), p. 222). On the other hand, he writes that for Newman 'if religion offers us a certainty, it is not certainty as the world understands it, but a certainty which is a mysterious fact to be taken far otherwise than the man of the world takes *his* certainties; as not certain at all by his criteria' (Ibid., p. 235). This implies that Newman did not think we could get speculative certainty in religion.

[50] 4 Nov. 1869 (cited by Zeno, *Our Way to Certitude*, p. 260).

[51] I find significant warrant in the *Critique of Practical Reason* and one strand in the *Critique of Pure Reason* for a claim that Kant's postulate of God postulates only the possibility and not the existence of God.

[52] *T.P.*, p. 35 (16 Dec. 1853).

Evidence is always incomplete, but sometimes it is sufficient for real certitude, . . . sometimes only for what is called practical certitude, i.e., what is prudent in action, . . .[53]

While it is sometimes only sufficient for practical certitude, it is sometimes, even in concrete cases, sufficient for real, total, speculative certitude. Newman clearly saw that 'acting as if' is not believing: 'No one would say we believed our house was on fire, because we thought it safest, on a cry of fire, to act as if it was.'[54] Newman's criticism of the effect, whether intended or not, of Butler's work shows that he thought that more than practical certainty was possible in religion.[55] He claimed explicitly that he did not think 'anyone *need* become a Catholic on merely practical certainty, none ought and I think very few do'.[56] He also noted defensively, in a letter to Dalgairns, that he used the term 'probable' in opposition to 'demonstrative' rather than to 'certain'.[57]

Newman distinguished practical certitude from 'speculative' or 'theoretic' certainty in the following way:

a man may be certain, as a practical point, that he ought to accept Scripture as the Word of God, though he be not certain, as a speculative matter, that it is such; and again he may [be] certain of its being his duty to perform acts of religion, whatever becomes of his doubts about the existence of a God. But speculative certainty, to be really such, must have a truth for its subject, and it must be a conviction of that truth.[58]

Speculative certainty is a conviction 'that a thing is actually true';[59] it implies earnestness about the subject-matter, and a reflex assent after deliberation, however rapid.[60] Such speculative certitude is the result of our natural personal faculty; we need not resign ourselves to less. It should be evident how superficial was Leslie Stephen's charge that Newman, 'having no trust in independent reason . . . justifies himself by the incongruous intervention of a supernatural authority'.[61]

On the whole it is clear that Newman saw the certitude of religious belief as more than practical — 'moral' did not, for him, mean 'practical' (318).[62] Such total speculative certainty

---

[53] *V.M. I*, p. 87, n.9; cf. *Apo.*, pp. 31-2.   [54] *V.M. I*, p. 87, n. 8.
[55] *T.P.*, p. 35, n. 1 (also *L.D.*, 15: 456).   [56] *T.P.*, p. 36 (16 Dec. 1853).
[57] *L.D.*, 11: 289 (8 Dec. 1846).   [58] *T.P.*, p. 128, (25 Sept. 1865).
[59] Ibid.   [60] Ibid., p. 35 (16 Dec. 1853).
[61] 'Newman's Theory of Belief', *An Agnostic's Apology*, p. 238.
[62] A somewhat problematical usage of the term 'moral certainty' is found in two of Newman's papers: there appears to be a conflict between the paper of April 1853 and December 1853.

is not, moreoever, the gift conferred in divine faith; such speculative certainty is possible to our natural reasoning processes. Newman wrote to Edward Healy Thompson in 1853:

It seems to be most clear, and in the experience of everyday, that we are positively and absolutely and speculativé (not practicé only) certain of a thing by a combination of arguments, each of which is only probable; and if so, why not in the case of Faith?[63]

There may indeed be a certainty peculiar to the faith that is a divine gift. But that does not mean that total speculative certainty is not possible on the basis of our reasoning processes. R. H. Hutton in an early commentary on Newman's thought reported Newman as believing that 'reasons which in themselves only amount to probabilities are often transformed into absolute certainty by the action of the Divine will'.[64] Speculative certainty, however, never depended for Newman on such a divine alchemical transformation.

In arguing for speculative certainty, Newman was at odds with men like Froude. As we noted earlier, according to Froude, practical certitude, a 'duty to *act as if* the conclusion . . . were absolutely certain' (his emphasis)[65] was all that was possible in either religion or science. To this Newman's response was:

You yourself allow that there are cases in which we are forced and have a duty to act, as if what is but possible were certainly true, as in our precautions against fire; I go further so much, not as to say that in merely possible, or simply probable cases, but in particular cases of the highest probability . . . it is a law of the human intellect . . . to accept with an inward assent as absolutely true, what is not yet demonstrated.[66]

Logical incompleteness does not relegate us to the realm of only practical certitude; not even the admission by a person that he would renounce his belief if the grounds were to fail him precludes the experience of speculative certitude in the meantime:

If some officious philosopher came, and told me that I must be prepared to give up my belief as soon as my grounds for believing went . . . and that it would be safer to take it as practically certain than

---

[63] *L.D.,* 15: 457 (7 Oct. 1853).

[64] R. H. Hutton, *Cardinal Newman* (Cambridge: The Riverside Press, 1890), pp. 20-1.

[65] Harper, p. 120 (29 Dec. 1853).   [66] Ibid., p. 203 (29 Apr. 1879).

speculatively, I should laugh in his face, and tell him that certainly I would renounce my belief . . . directly that any ground for believing failed me, but not till then.[67]

This speculative certainty is reached through our capacity for right judgement in informal reasoning. Newman explored the reaches of informal reasoning, and he did not find it wanting.

The preceding discussion has approached the question of the will in certitude somewhat obliquely. Looking back now we can see that for Newman the view that our experience must be elevated 'into something more than it is in itself' if we are to avoid scepticism, effectively canonizes an analytic paradigm of certainty quite as much as does the sceptical conclusion itself. And neither is necessary because the analytic paradigm is not the sole provider of epistemological salvation. Since it is not, the experience of certitude need not be the result of an artificial gap-bridging by the will. But how then do we fulfil a 'duty to be certain'; in what way is certitude a 'free act' which depends on the will?

[67] *T.P.*, pp. 5–6. (14 Apr. 1853).

CHAPTER

III

> Certainty is an act (habit) of the intellect reflecting on, recognising, and ratifying its existing apprehension of a truth.
>
> JHN, 16 December 1853

> ... the act of certitude is a *certifying* it or giving a *certificate* which henceforth will be its passport and protection.
>
> JHN, 20 July 1865

Newman's general view of the limits and achievements of reasoning processes provides significant warrant for the conclusion that he did not see the need for any gap-filler. We can now directly approach some of the crucial texts on the will and certainty to see how these specific texts can support and be supported by the considerations in the preceding chapter, as well as how they shed further light on the positive role of the will. In general I shall be arguing that the full extent of Newman's views on religious commitment and its relation to doubt cannot be appreciated until a careful distinction is drawn between two different roles of the will with respect to certitude. In Newman's thought the will comes into play at different times and in different ways — first, in the process of reaching certitude and second, in confirming an already experienced certitude. The role of 'choice' with respect to each role is different; when these two roles are confused or conflated, justice cannot be done to Newman's thought. In the attempt to do justice to this distinction, we shall further our understanding of the concepts of 'free decision' and 'objectivity' in Newman's account, thus contributing indirectly to the problem of 'the will to believe'.

1. Certitude: Experience and Confirmation

The variety in Newman's descriptions of certitude has already been indicated. The ambiguity that arises is especially striking in Newman's paper of 13 May 1853. Here the ambiguity is not between contrasting passages, but within single paragraphs. One gets the impression that each succeeding phrase is unexpected, counteracting the previous one rather than elaborating it. For example:

> Upon an inference of whatever kind there is *a natural spontaneous act of the mind* toward it of acceptance or the reverse, which I have above expressed under the word Assent, and said to be *under the jurisidiction of the will*. . . . And if the inference be (demonstrated or) really proved, or a conviction, then a very special acceptance or *recognition* of it will take place . . . which acceptance is called certainty.[1]

Assent, and *a fortiori* certitude as a reflex assent, is an 'acceptance' which is under the 'jurisdiction of the will'. Yet it is also a 'spontaneous act of the mind'. Newman seems to be saying both that the acceptance is a spontaneous act and that it is a deliberate act. The word 'acceptance' is ambiguous and can have both meanings, so it does not, in itself, help us to determine Newman's intention.

The same ambiguity is repeated a page later in the paper, where he writes:

> This certainty, which though it *naturally follows upon* conviction, is a making up the mind that a thing is true which is proved, and *therefore is under the control of the will*.[2]

How can something 'naturally follow' yet be 'under the control of the will'? To determine precisely what Newman means by the control of the will it is necessary to consider the passages just cited in more detail. For example, Newman immediately follows up his claim that certainty is under the control of the will by explaining:

> That is, the will may suppress, extinguish the feeling . . . . The will cannot absolutely create it, for it is the natural and direct result of conviction, but the will can hinder that direct result [from] taking place. . . . The will, then, though it cannot create ⟨force⟩ certainty, can stifle it.[3]

This does not resolve the issue, however, since the claim that

---

[1] *T.P.*, p. 14 (13 May 1853). Emphasis mine.
[2] *T.P.*, p. 15 (13 May 1853). Emphasis mine.
[3] Ibid.; words in arrow brackets indicate Newman's own interlinear additions.

'the will can hinder that direct result [*from*] *taking place*'
seems to conflict with the remainder of the passage. The
point of the entire passage could be either of two things:

> (A) The will can prevent certainty from arising at all. That
> is, the will can prevent the natural result of convic-
> tion, the feeling of assurance, from taking place, from
> being experienced,

or

> (B) The will cannot prevent the experience of certainty,
> though it can stifle or extinguish it.

Newman's claim a few lines later that we can 'refuse to be
certain'[4] can therefore mean either that we (A) can refuse
to experience certainty at all, or (B) can refuse to *abide by*
the certainty we in fact experience; we can refuse to confirm
it or we can attempt to undermine it.

Accordingly, the 'jurisdiction of the will' can be interpreted
as referring to (A) a refusal actually to accept (i.e. experience)
proposition *p* without reservation, or (B) a refusal to accept
(i.e. confirm) my spontaneous acceptance-without-reserva-
tion. The crucial thing to note is that if Newman means that
we can refuse to be certain in sense (A), we obversely must
have to *choose* to experience complete assurance. Sense (A)
of refusing to be certain provides one way of interpreting
Newman's claim that an act of certitude can be made in response to perceived duty. However, it flatly contradicts
Newman's explicit claim that the will cannot create or force
certainty. Sense (B) offers us a way of reconciling the idea of
control of the will with the idea of the spontaneity of
certitude. Of the two possible roles of the will — creating and
stifling certitude — it seems that Newman's clearest statements support a denial of the former. Control of the will
would therefore refer to a critical function of the will.[5]

Another way of phrasing the alternative understandings of
the role of the will in certitude is to consider the following
set of distinctions, which highlight the ambiguity in the
judgement of 'acceptance':

> (1) judgement that I *ought to accept* proposition *p* with-
> out reservation,

---

[4] Ibid.
[5] Cf. *U.S.*, X, p. 183, on the 'critical' rather than 'creative' role of reason.

    (2)   actual experience (acceptance) of *p* without reserva-
          tion,
    (3)   consequent intellectual confirmation (acceptance)
          following experience.

Let us assume that Newman intends the judgement that I
ought. to *accept* to be equivalent to the judgement that I
ought to *experience p* as certain. When certitude is seen as
something we can refuse to experience or need to choose to
experience, the experience (2) is separated from the judgement (1). On this model a separate act over and above the
judgement is thought to be necessary; implicit is the assumption that to judge that we ought not to have any reservations
is not *in itself* to experience no reservation. On the other
hand, the claim that there is no gap which has to be bridged
by a choice identifies the illative judgement with the actual
experience. On this model, the judgement that we ought to
accept something without reservation is a *de facto* experience
of it without reservation. The very judgement is that although
we could possibly have had reservations because the matter
is not logically demonstrated, we do not in fact experience
any. The process of reasoning has led to a state in which no
such reservations are felt. Though we can decide not to act
according to the lack of reservation we may in a given case
experience (i.e. we may decide not to confirm our certitude),
it does not make sense to say that we can choose not to
experience reservations. If we judge that we would be idiotic
not to accept the proposition without reservation, we have
effectively experienced the proposition without reservation.
What is still possible, of course, is to refuse to abide by or
confirm the certainty we feel; we can choose to stifle it. In
such a model, therefore, the role of the will would be that of
confirmation or negation; this model, rather than the former,
would be consistent with the conclusion noted earlier that
Newman's clearest statements support the critical, rather
than the creative role of the will.

    The previous chapter exhibited the main support for opting
for this understanding of Newman's position — i.e. Newman's
rejection of an analytic paradigm and his understanding of
the extents of informal reasoning militate against the idea of
a separation between the illative judgement and actual

experience of certitude, against the idea of a gap to be filled in by 'choice'. In the remainder of this chapter I shall discuss two other considerations which reinforce or illustrate this conclusion. The first involves a 'moral analogy', and the second involves the elaboration of the implications of Newman's rejection of an analytic paradigm with respect to freedom and constraint.

A. The Moral Analogy

Newman's claim that we go 'after the proof, to an act of certitude', and that when we have a duty to be certain we should fulfil that duty,[6] might be thought to suggest that Newman saw the experience of p without reservation as distinct from the judgement that we ought to experience it without reservation. Newman clearly conceived of being certain in a moral idiom, and one explanation for a separation of judgement of acceptance from actual experience of certitude (and hence for the need of a 'choice') might be that Newman was misled by the superficial structure of the standard moral analogy. At first glance there is indeed an un-problematical distinction between a judgement that I ought to do X (i.e. have a duty to do X) and the fulfilment of that duty. To judge that I ought to go to the market is not in it-self to go to the market. To judge that I ought to accept X does not seem to be identical with actually accepting X; there seems to be room for and need of an act over and above the judgement.

But this is to misread the moral analogy. Even in the standard moral case, there is no distinction between the judgement and the acceptance, though there is indeed a distinction between the acceptance and the consequence of it. That is, the judgement that I ought to do X is itself already a judgement that X is right (good) to do; it is already an acceptance of the claim that X is right to do. I have no choice about that acceptance once the judgement is made. The judgement need not be logically compelling; all sorts of personal considerations may enter into an assessment of the case. But the fact that it is not logically compelled does not

---

[6] *G.A.*, p. 329; *T.P.*, p. 121 (1865).

mean that I can, at the point of judging, 'freely' choose to accept or reject what the judgement itself consists in. I have that kind of free choice only about what I shall *do* about that judgement I have come to, for I can certainly judge something to be right to do and still refuse to act on it.[7]

The standard moral analogy rightly understood does seem to hold for the parallel problem of an intellectual judgement and the stifling or confirming of it. Choice does not come in to bring about an acceptance (i.e. experience) after the judgemet; the judgement *is* the intellectual acceptance which can be followed by practical affirmation or negation of that acceptance. In other words, the separation supported by the standard moral analogy is the separation of ought-judgement from confirmation of experienced certitude, not the separation of ought-judgement from experience of certitude. In so far as Newman intended 'I ought to accept *p* as certain' to mean 'I ought to experience *p* as certain', the duty analogy provides no basis for a gap.

Was Newman actually confused about the relation between the ought-judgement and the actual experience of certitude? The fact that he *need not* have separated the two on the basis of a duty analogy provides some evidence (though certainly not conclusive evidence, since he may have *thought* he needed to) against the view that he separated them. By far the stronger reason, however, for denying the separation can be found in the rejection, outlined earlier, of the intellectual position which provides the motive for such a separation. Since Newman did not see a gap to be bridged, his judgement that I ought to be certain or ought to accept *p* as certain is equivalent in his Victorian idiom to an experience of certitude. That it might not immediately seem equivalent to us is perhaps due in part to our post-Victorian disinclination to construe judgements of 'fact' in moral terms, and perhaps to our being misled by the surface structure of the standard moral analogy. We can now turn to the implications of Newman's rejection of an analytic paradigm.

---

[7] Another view of 'weakness of will' might conflate the judgement and confirmation, but it need not separate the judgement and the experience unless one built in certain restrictions on the context of judgement.

B. The Analytic Paradigm — A Reappraisal

The motive for resolving the ambiguity concerning the distinction between illative judgement and unconditional acceptance in favour of an actual separation of the two lies in a particular understanding of the character of 'non-entailment', an understanding which manifests an uncritical adherence to an analytic paradigm of reasoning.

Newman saw arguments as capable of being conclusive for the same reason Toulmin suggests:

Certainly analytic arguments alone are analytic — and so, in the professional logician's sense 'conclusive'; but in other fields also a time comes when we have produced in support of our conclusions data and warrants full and strong enough, in the context, for further investigation to be unnecessary — so in this sense non-analytic arguments can also be conclusive.[8]

This is another way of phrasing one of Newman's favourite ideas: *in context* twelve pieces of evidence or twelve witnesses can generate total certainty; it is foolish therefore to maintain that since a thirteenth *could* be added one should not be without doubt on the basis of the twelve. That is, it is foolish to say that since there could be more than twelve one should cherish reservations solely in deference to the space between twelve and however many might be possible.[9] In this way Newman used a distinction which is still thought necessary to emphasize today: namely, the distinction between 'conclusiveness' and 'incorrigibility'.[10]

Where, however, analytic demonstration is seen as the sole source of total certainty, the distinction between the entailment of certainty and the non-entailment of certainty becomes a stark division, a black-and-white contrast between *compulsion* and *freedom*. Either we are coerced by the argument or we simply choose what we prefer to believe.[11] Free assent, on such a view, is an arbitrary assent. Although Newman does at one point call assent an 'arbitrary' act (188), a simplistic contrast between compulsion and freedom is not

---

[8] Toulmin, *Uses of Argument*, p. 234.   [9] *T.P.*, p. 124 (20 July 1865).

[10] Cf. Douglas Greenlea, 'Unrestricted Fallibilism', *Trans. C.S. Peirce Soc.* 7 (Apr. 1971), p. 76.

[11] Cf. Pailin, *The Way to Faith*, p. 177: 'we cannot be coerced to assent by any force of argument; finally our act of assent is a matter of personal decision'.

part of Newman's view of non-entailment. In the following sections I will consider how Newman sees the relation between freedom and constraint, as well as how he sees the relation of 'personal' to 'objective'.

i. Freedom and Constraint   What Newman means by non-entailment of certitude can be gathered indirectly. He opposes 'passive impression made upon the mind from without, by argumentative compulsion' to an 'active recognition of propositions as true' (344, 345).[12] He claims that 'certitude then is not the passive admission of a conclusion as necessary, but the recognition of it as true . . . the act of certitude is a *certifying* it'.[13] Newman does see non-entailment as precluding compulsion and passive impression, but he proposes another category in between those extremes and a simple 'choice'. He makes us aware of the value of the content of the category of 'active recognition'. Rephrased in a Wittgensteinian idiom, certitude is a 'taking hold'.[14] But what does the 'active' character of an 'active recognition' consist in?

First, Newman requires that assent and certitude be a free act for which the doer is responsible (232), and that certitude be a free act just as the acts of our conscience are free.[15] On the other hand, Newman's descriptions of the force of the conclusions testify to his belief that non-entailment does not mean that the conclusion is not constraining.[16] He says, as we saw earlier, that we would be idiotic not to accept the conclusion; a man would be irrational to doubt it; the conclusion cannot be otherwise; it is one that should be accepted by all wise men.[17] It is, moreover, a 'law of my mind to seal up conclusions to which ratiocination has brought me, by that

---

[12] Cf. *T.P.*, p. 31 (16 Dec. 1853).   [13] *T.P.*, p. 126 (20 July 1865).
[14] Wittgenstein, *On Certainty*, eds. G. E. M. Anscombe and G. H. von Wright (New York: Harper & Row, 1969), § 511.   [15] *T.P.*, p. 121 (1865).
[16] However much Newman might have shared a common tradition with Coleridge (cf. John Coulson, *Newman and the Common Tradition* (Oxford: Clarendon Press, 1970)), he may have differed in this respect. Coleridge seems, like Kierkegaard, to have valued objective uncertainty in a way that Newman does not; the value of things does not decrease for Newman in proportion as they become 'intellectually more evident' (cf. Coleridge's *Biographia Literaria*, ed. J. Shawcross (Oxford: Clarendon Press, 1970), 1:135–56).
[17] This last phrase is referred to by Newman, quoting from Huet, *Dev.*, p. 334.

formal assent which I have called a certitude. I could indeed
have withheld my assent, but I should have acted against my
nature' (229). The 'correlative of ascertained truth is un-
reserved assent' (170). The act of certitude 'being then of a
personal character, not the necessary effect . . . of antecedents
of the ⟨a⟩ scientific character . . . not elicited of necessity by
the intrinsic force of argument'[18] is not impersonally compelled by arguments. The conclusion is not reached 'by a
scientific necessity independent of ourselves', but the
'individual perception of the truth' is still ruled by 'a sense
of duty to those conclusions' (318). Newman, therefore,
distinguished between impersonal compulsion and personal
constraint, between the compulsion of a logical deduction
and the constraint of a rational evaluation.

Individual men will come to questions with varying antecedent assumptions: the 'cumulation of probabilities . . . will
vary both in their number and their separate estimated value,
according to the particular intellect which is employed upon
it' (293). What constitutes a proof for one man will not for
another (293). But that is not to say that if two men went
through substantially the same informal reasoning process
they could each reasonably come to opposite conclusions —
'a proof is something such that it can only be on *one* side'.[19]
The freedom Newman requires, characterizing non-entailment, is not arbitrary (we shall develop this further in the
next section); the constraint of a rational evaluation or assessment of evidence is not incompatible with such freedom.

Assent can be adequately free if the entire process of
coming to the conclusion is one of personal evaluation. The
freedom Newman requires is provided for by the recognition
that it is the individual who reasons, with all his antecedent
assumptions. Assent and certitude are not dragged forth
from the individual against his will — the reflex assent,
Newman says, 'cannot ⟨is not⟩ be done without ⟨against⟩ the
will' [*sic*][20] — but neither is it bestowed as a result of a
choice based on our desires. The 'bald syllogism' does not
compel in concrete matters, yet a particular assent can be
required of all wise or reasonable men. The force comes

---

[18] *T.P.*, p. 126 (20 July 1865).   [19] *L.D.*, 14:348 (7 Sept. 1857).
[20] *T.P.*, p. 130 (4 Aug. 1866).

from a personal evaluation.

One can properly speak of an 'active recognition' or judgement as a *decision*, since it is not entailed or compelled. But, to use a standard distinction, it is a 'decision-that-X' rather than a 'decision-to-do-X'.[21] Deciding that X is certain is different from deciding to do X; it is different, therefore, from deciding to affirm X as certain, even though one does not experience it as certain. The popular use of the word 'decide' must not be allowed to obscure that distinction since it is crucial in Newman's case. The 'personal' element in Newman's view of right reasoning does not imply 'personal' judgement in the way that my decision to go to the market is a personal one. An active recognition may be a decision, for which a person is responsible, but it need not be a decision of the same sort as my decision to go to the market.

A decision-that-X-is-certain is equivalent to experiencing X as certain.[22] A judgement or decision about the existence of a matter of fact or state of affairs clearly differs from a judgement or decision *to* initiate an action or state of affairs. But what about a decision that I *ought to be certain* that X? Are all ought-judgements arbitrary?

It is important to show that not all ought-judgements are of the same kind. Judgements of the type 'I ought to be certain that X' are different in crucial respects from judgements of the type 'I ought to go to the market'. In the latter case the assessment is made at least in part (and legitimately) on the basis of an individual's needs and desires and interests. True, some purely existential judgements that A, B and C are the case might be involved, but the judgement that 'I ought to go to the market' depends on my preferences in a way that the judgement that the market is fifty yards away, for example, does not. The judgement or 'decision-that-X' (or in Newman's case, the decision-that-I-ought-to-be-certain-that-X, since both equal the experience that X is certain) depends at

---

[21] *Encyclopedia of Philosophy*, reprint ed. 1972, s.v. 'Choosing , Deciding and Doing', by Andrew Oldenquist.

[22] Stuart Hampshire, *Thought and Action* (London: Chatto & Windus, 1959), p. 155. Also cf. Richard Aaron, in *Knowing and the Function of Reason* (Oxford: Clarendon Press, 1971) contrasts 'being sure' and 'making a decision' by characterizing a decision simply as the 'choosing freely between alternatives', p. 57.

least normatively and ideally on the *categorical* end of truth-seeking (though not necessarily in a Kantian sense of categorical as transcending all human interests). It would be considered a failing to let such a judgement be guided consciously by personal preference. In judging that I ought to go to the market, however, needs and desires can be legitimate (and even sufficient) factors to be considered.

The importance of Newman's claim to non-entailment of certitude lies in the emphasis on the personal, active character of certitude as opposed to passive, impersonal compulsion. Because the entire reasoning process is a personal one, an emphasis on freedom does not imply the need for a totally arbitrary choice. The active recognition or decision by an individual does not imply either the kind of freedom involved in a decision to go to the market, or the kind involved in a judgement that I ought to go to the market. The active recognition that constitutes certitude can be a decision in that it is not compelled; it is nevertheless a decision constrained by a process of rational assessment of evidence, and constrained in a way that not all ought-judgements are.

ii Objectivity and the Arbitrary   Newman has been criticized for confusing 'the objectively logical with the subjectively personal'.[23] This criticism illustrates the illegitimate and simplistic opposition of freedom and compulsion which I have just suggested Newman did not share. It also leads us to consider in more detail what 'objectivity' means for Newman and how it relates to the requirement that reasoning is *personal*. I suggest that Newman is offering a deepened view of objectivity, with some contemporary-sounding presuppositions and implications.

Newman argued that his admission that 'what to one intellect is a proof is not so to another' did *not* 'prejudice . . . the objective truth or falsehood of propositions' (293). This reveals the tension between the concepts of 'personal' and 'objective'. Newman's reminder that proof is in some sense person-dependent was not meant to imply that certitude is dependent on what each man thinks is certain since Newman's avowed intention was to 'lessen the difficulties which lie in

[23] Pailin, *The Way to Faith*, p. 185; Newman's contemporaries also found this a major criticism.

the way of calling [someone] to account for [claims to certainty]' (196). Thus Newman seems to have believed that 'personal' need not be opposed to 'objective'.

One way of explicating such a view is suggested by a discussion of rationality by Robert Solomon.[24] Solomon suggests that rationality should be understood as indifferent to *particular* persons. What is rational is not determined by individual whim or caprice — it is *not* 'person-relative'. Yet a belief 'may be rational for one person at one time and not for another and/or at another time' — it is 'person-variable'.[25] This lack of 'person-relativity' is reconciled with the need for 'person-variability' by distinguishing between what is independent of any particular consciousness and what is independent of every consciousness. Rationality can be indifferent to particular persons, yet objective because relative to epistemic communities, groups which share significantly overlapping belief systems.

Is there any support for such a position in Newman's work? In an early essay republished by him in 1871, Newman argued for the objectivity of religious truth, and apparently accepted the following definition of 'Objective Truth':

By Objective Truth is meant the Religious System considered as existing in itself, external to this or that particular mind.[26]

It seems, then, that for Newman 'objective' need not bear a Kantian sense — it need not transcend humanness as such. Objectivity might require only that the judgement in question transcend 'this or that particular mind'.

Newman expanded on the subject of Objective Truth as follows:

To believe in Objective Truth is to throw ourselves forward upon that which we have but partially mastered or made subjective; to embrace, maintain, and use general proportions which are larger than our own capacity, of which we cannot see the bottom, which we cannot follow out into their multiform details; to come before and bow before the import of such propositions, as if we were contemplating what is real and independent of human judgment.[27]

On the one hand, Newman is claiming that Objective Truth is

---

[24] 'God and Rationality', *Canadian Journal of Philosophy* 4 (Dec. 1974).

[25] Ibid., p. 285; cf. also *Charles S. Peirce: Selected Writings*, 'How To Make Our Ideas Clear', p. 133.

[26] *Ess.*, 1:34.   [27] Ibid.

greater than 'this or that particular mind', but on the other hand he is claiming that we bow before general propositions as if independent of human judgement. A crucial aspect of this latter phrase, however, is the 'as if'. These selections, therefore, both suggest that Newman *could* have admitted that 'objective' truth need not actually be independent of human judgement as such. He need not require, for objectivity, a necessary correspondence with absolute truth-values existing independently of human judgement.

Although Newman would certainly not have seen 'objective' truth as relative to anything less than the entire human community, the basic principle of Solomon's distinction does seem to offer a plausible way of understanding Newman's claim that judgements of certitude are both personal and objective. Such a distinction seems to fit in quite well with the claim that 'objective' refers to what is external to 'this or that particular mind'. The rationality of a judgement of certainty in such a case would be personal, because not independent of every consciousness (or human consciousness as such) yet objective because independent of particular consciousnesses.[28]

This discussion raises the related issue of description and prescription in Newman's work since it too involves the question of 'objectivity'.

Newman makes two claims which might lead to the conclusion that he restricts his concern to psychological description without regard to legitimacy or justification.[29] First, in a letter to Froude Newman wrote:

We differ in our sense and our use of the word 'certain'. I use it of minds, you of propositions. I fully grant the uncertainty of all conclusions in your sense of the word, but I maintain that minds may in

---

[28] If it is suggested that being 'personal' necessarily makes it 'subjective', then there is no certainty that is not subjective; it is always personally appropriated to some degree. Cf. *Encyclopedia of Philosophy*, reprint ed. 1972, s.v. 'Certainty' by C. D. Rollins: 'certainty of propositions requires psychological certainty plus its justification'. Cf. also D. M. Armstrong, *Belief, Truth and Knowledge* (Cambridge: University Press, 1973), p. 139.

[29] C. S. Dessain, 'Cardinal Newman on the Theory and Practice of Knowledge' argues that 'Newman ... deals with his problem as a psychological one, not as an epistemological one', p. 16. This could be misleading if taken to mean that Newman is only doing psychological description as opposed to justification. Dessain himself does not make this error.

my sense be certain of conclusions which are uncertain in yours.[30]
Was Newman's sense a purely subjective one? Was he giving
up a claim to objective certainty? A second passage may help
us to determine this.

In the *Grammar* Newman warned that when philosophers
tell us that our assents ought to be proportioned to the inferential reasoning preceding them

are they not to be considered as confusing together two things very
distinct from each other, a mental act or state and a scientific rule, an
interior assent and a set of logical formulas? When they speak of
degrees of assent, surely they have no intention at all of defining the
position of the mind itself relative to the adoption of a given conclusion, but they are recording their perception of the relation of that
conclusion towards its premisses. (179-80)

Newman therefore opposes both the 'mental state' of certainty
to a 'scientific rule' and the certainty of minds to the certainty of propositions. I suggest that both passages can best
be interpreted in light of the previous discussion of Newman's
rejection of an analytic paradigm. The 'scientific rule' or 'set
of formulas', like propositional certainty, refers to logic in a
limited sense, an independent quality of propositions. The
'mental state' would refer to the personal appropriation of
the certainty. The 'scientific rule' involves semantic relations
between premisses and conclusions; the 'mental state' is an
appropriation through personal reasoning.

The distinction, therefore, between 'mental state' and
'scientific rule' or quality of propositions need not be
Newman's way of limiting himself to pure description without regard to justification. It is, rather, another expression of
his claim that certainty is. not exhausted by a logical
paradigm. He is not necessarily separating mental state from
evidential justification, but rather suggesting that the mental
state of certainty is not only justified when it results from
recognition of analytic relations between premisses and conclusions. There are two sources of certainty — both are entire;
certainty attaches to demonstration as well as to some substantial arguments.

Several other claims made by Newman also seem to be
rejections of a normative inquiry. He says: 'my only business
is to ascertain what I am, in order to put it to use' (347). Any

[30] Harper, p. 201 (29 Apr. 1879).

interest in 'how it comes about that we can be certain' (344) is disavowed, since it is enough for him that certitude is felt; his aim is simply to determine the 'matter of fact' about when assent is given to propositions which are inferred (343). Newman's intentions to describe, however, need not be a rejection of a normative concern, since they are contrasted by him with particular kinds of enterprises — e.g. *explanatory* psychological account (343-4), or an *a priori* normative account (216, 344). The emphases on description need not conflict with a non-*a priori* normative account. In such a case the ethics language in the *Grammar,* the concern with what processes 'legitimately' lead to assent, need not be seen as contradicting the apparently purely descriptive intentions. But what would be the status of such a non-*a priori* normative account? Is Newman incorrectly conflating prescription with description?

In rejecting the need for transcendental gap-fillers Newman replied that it was enough to appeal to the 'normal operation of our nature'. He explained:

That is to be accounted a normal operation of our nature, which men in general do actually instance. That is a law of our minds, which is exemplified in action on a large scale, whether *a priori* it ought to be a law or no. (344)

Newman is claiming that the determinination about the 'matter of fact' about when assent is given, as well as ascertaining what we are, involve the determination of the laws under which we live.[31] Those laws are not rules that exist independently of human judgement as such. Normative judgements about 'right reasoning' depend on information about how men in fact generally reason. In effect, Newman is suggesting that it does not really make sense to ask whether or not something '*a priori*' ought to be a law of reasoning.

One way of approaching this aspect of Newman's thought is suggested by the twentieth-century discussions initiated by Wittgenstein and Quine. My use of these philosophers should be prefaced with a few words of caution. First, my reference to their thought is not meant to suggest that they and Newman do exactly the same thing. There are significant

---

[31] *G.A.,* p. 347; cf. Ward II, p. 248 (letter to Wilberforce, 1868): '*It is a law of our nature,* then that we are certain on premisses which do not reach demonstration.'

differences and I attempt to remain sensitive to these. Secondly, the use of Wittgenstein is particularly problematical. This is due to two factors: (a) the difficulty in understanding Wittgenstein's thought in itself; and (b) the difficulty in dissociating it from the use to which it has been put by some religious thinkers. Since I do not think that Wittgenstein's later work entails a 'fideist' religious understanding,[32] my reference to him is not meant to provide support for a 'fideist' interpretation of Newman's thought. With these caveats and qualifications made, I can return to a brief summary of those twentieth-century discussions which I hope can illuminate in some respects Newman's view of the relation between description and prescription with respect to epistemological standards.

Wittgenstein and Quine remind us that the status of 'necessary' or 'certain' is a function of centrality in our web of beliefs. The context according to which reasonableness, necessity, or certainty is determined is a system of beliefs (or a world picture), made plausible as a totality, dialectically issuing from and informing a way of life.[33] The legitimacy of judgements of certainty depends on what beliefs are crucial to a given community, and this cannot be determined *a priori*. Claims about what we know with certainty are embedded in this frame of reference we share.[34]

Some beliefs are at the core of this world picture and abandonment of them would result in chaotic disruption of the entire system of beliefs.[35] We could not abandon them

---

[32] Support for this conclusion can be found in the following sources: Patrick Sherry's *Religion, Truth and Language-Games* (Macmillan, 1977) as well as Sherry's article 'Is Religion a "Form of Life"?' *American Philosophical Quarterly* 9 (Apr. 1972); J. F. M. Hunter's article, 'Forms of Life in Wittgenstein's *Philosophical Investigations*', *American Philosophical Quarterly* 5 (Oct. 1968). Also see *Wittgenstein and Knowledge: The Importance of On Certainty* by Thomas Morawetz (Amherst, Mass.: University of Massachusetts Press, 1978), pp. 108, 119–37.

[33] Wittgenstein, *On Certainty*, § § 94, 105, 140; cf. also *The Web of Belief* by W. V. O. Quine and J. S. Ullian.

[34] Wittgenstein's *On Certainty* § 83; cf. *Philosophical Investigations*, trans. G. E. M. Anscombe (New York: Macmillan Co., 1968), No. 50. See also John Coulson, *Newman and the Common Tradition*, for a somewhat different approach to the question of the relation of language and society in Newman. Coulson does not reach my conclusions, but I think his suggestions provide a specific instance of my own. [35] *On Certainty* § § 492, 613.

and continue to make any claims at all. Others are more peripheral, and can be relinquished more easily.[36] The boundaries between 'hard' and 'fluid' propositions, between the river bed and the waters that flow on the river, are not static; the same proposition can be a test at one time and what is tested at another.[37] This is precisely because these judgements are human determinations. Hacker describes the Wittgensteinian view in the following way:

Concept formation is part of the constitution of a world-picture. The formation of a concept guides our experience into particular channels, determining the ways in which we see things. . . . According to Wittgenstein's constructivist philosophy it is something we accept or reject, it is never forced upon us. In as much as we accept it, it guides our experience into particular channels. For the acceptance of a proof and the consequent sacrosanctity of the resultant theorem . . . is simply a determination to treat the theorem, as Brouwer has suggested we treat the laws of logic, as unassailable by experience. Moreover, the unassailability is normative not factual.[38]

The concepts and 'empirical' propositions which constitute our world picture are determinations to channel our experience in particular ways. These determinations, moreover, are not the discovery of metaphysical matters of fact — they are constructive judgements which are normative. There is no other source for norms.

An important qualification needs to be made here concerning the normative aspects of Wittgenstein's account. Wittgenstein is concerned, in general, to deny the need for justification of particular practices rather than to offer another view of what constitutes justification for them. He is not offering another answer to the same old question — he is challenging the sense of the request for justification. Wittgenstein offers a description of the way norms are generated, but his description is not put forth as normative; there is no attempt to justify or legitimate one thing rather than another. Newman, on the contrary, does seem to want to legitimate or sanction practices: 'it is enough for the proof of the value and authority of any function which I possess, to be able to pronounce that

[36] W. V. O. Quine, 'Two Dogmas of Empiricism', in *From a Logical Point of View,* 2nd ed. (New York: Harper Torchbooks, 1963), esp. pp. 42–3.

[37] *On Certainty,* § § 96–8.

[38] P. M. S. Hacker, *Insight and Illusion* (Oxford: Clarendon Press, 1972), pp. 148–9.

it is natural' (347). The difference can be expressed in terms of Newman's claim that 'our hoping is a proof that hope, as such, is not an extravagance' (344): Newman seems to see the practice as justified thereby, while Wittgenstein would see the practice as thereby relieved of the need for justification.[39] It should be noted at this point that there is a difference between attempting to justify a practice as such, and attempting to provide an automatic justification for any particular instance of the practice. Newman need not be attempting to justify any given instance of hoping or being certain by his reference to the validity of either general practice.

Wittgenstein's usual response to the search for justification is simply to say 'This is how we do it.' However, sometimes rather than abruptly stopping there he goes on to imply 'This is what we do *because* . . .' — because of the way we are constituted or because something external to us is as it is. Wittgenstein admits that if 'we imagine the facts otherwise then as they are' certain practices will lose their importance.[40] If we imagine things in the world acting radically differently,[41] or if we imagine certain 'very general facts of nature to be different from what we are used to . . . the formation of concepts different from the usual ones will become intelligible' to us.[42] It is in this respect that I think Newman's thought can be illuminated by reference to Wittgenstein.

The relation between constructivism (or the importance of convention) and objectivity is expressed by Wittgenstein in terms of the tension between 'arbitrary' and 'non-arbitrary'. The arbitrariness Wittgenstein assumes is the arbitrariness of constitutive rules — the 'laws of the mind' are not things external to and independent of human judgement, things to which we need to conform. The rules of 'right reasoning' are constitutive; they are not descriptions of *a priori* laws.[43] But the rules are non-arbitrary in that they are neither capricious

---

[39] Cf. *Philosophical Investigations* No. 23 where Wittgenstein talks about the language games of 'asking, thanking, cursing, greeting, praying', as well as Sherry's remark in this respect ('Is Religion a "Form of Life"?').

[40] *On Certitude* §. 63.   [41] *Philosophical Investigations* No. 142.

[42] Ibid., p. 230.

[43] Ibid., No. 497; also cf. Hacker, *Insight and Illusion*, pp. 174-5.

nor individualistic, but rather social. The non-arbitrariness is also, as noted above, a function of the constancy of both external nature and human nature. Hacker, for example, suggests that for Wittgenstein changes in physiology and psychology would 'cause or prompt conceptual change . . . our psychological concepts would have no application if human behavioral responses to internal and external states were not — as a brute fact of nature — shared, regular and relatively uniform'.[44]

Newman is not basing norms on individual appraisals; intellectual morality is indifferent to particular minds. Judgements are formed collectively; norms about right reasoning and judgements of certainty are relative to the human epistemic community. It should be noted of course that for Newman the human community or language game referred to could be nothing less than the entire human community with the constitution given it by God. The understanding of what is implied in 'human nature' may well differ, but the basic idea that judgements of certainty are tied to ways of living seems to underlie Newman's thought quite as much as Wittgenstein's. Further support for this conclusion will be discussed in Chapter V, Section 3.

In sum: Newman, unlike Wittgenstein, does attempt to justify practices, but like Wittgenstein he questions whether it really makes sense to ask whether something '*a priori*' ought to be a law of reasoning. Newman is basing normative judgements on empirical judgements in the sense of claiming both that non-*a priori* normative inquiry is the only sort possible, and that such an inquiry reveals objective norms.

2. Two Roles of the Will: Recognition and Commitment

Detailed consideration of the implications of Newman's rejection of an analytic paradigm, focusing on the relation of constraint and freedom, reinforces the claim made earlier that Newman did not separate the judgement that one ought to be certain that p from the experience of p as certain, though he did separate the experience from the consequent confirmation or stifling of the experienced certitude. This

---

[44] Hacker, *Insight and Illusion*, p. 170.

points to two distinct roles of the will which must be kept in mind when reading Newman's thought on certitude. An interpretation of Newman's thought according to which certitude is reached by a choice or arbitrary decision, neither expresses Newman's general position on how certitude is reached, nor expresses a vacillation or contradiction in his thought. Such an interpretation either misunderstands the role of the will in reaching certitude or confuses it with another crucial aspect of Newman's thought on certitude — namely, the role of the will in affirming an already experienced certitude.

It must be repeated that Newman himself admitted his work on certainty in the *Grammar* was not definitive. Since the *Grammar* was his mature formulation, such a qualification would undoubtedly also apply to the papers preceding the *Grammar*. Newman's comment on the *Grammar* — that it is 'certainly characterized by incompleteness and crudeness'[45] — is therefore true of all the texts we have considered thus far, but I suggest that they nevertheless make a significant contribution to discussions of the relation between willing and certainty. Since that relation is difficult to grasp and even more difficult to express, Newman's attempts lack consistent clarity and are sometimes misleading. In distinguishing these two roles of the will as I do I am attempting to clarify what I see as important insights in Newman's thought on certainty.

The two roles of the will to which I see Newman pointing can be summarized under two main headings: Certitude as Active Recognition and Certitude as Deliberate Commitment. While both are important, the second deserves more emphasis since it has tended to be ignored or confused with the first role. The possibility of a third role with respect to a divine gift of faith will be considered in the final chapter.

A. *Active Recognition: The Role of the Will in REACHING Certitude*

Certitude is not reached through a choice distinct from the reasoning process, but is an active, uncompelled yet constrained recognition. Given that Newman is using 'faculty'

---

[45] Ward II, pp. 270-1.

terminology, it is not surprising that he would speak of the personal contributions to the entire reasoning process as 'acts of will'. These, however, refer to acts meaningfully done, as opposed to passive, reflexive, or compelled reactions. What Newman is anxious to point out is that reasoning is not impersonal or compelled; we do not assent or become certain *without* or *against* the will. Newman's reference to the will also undoubtedly refers to the 'willing nature' William James highlights — the passional input, the 'factors of belief' which complement our purely intellectual nature.[46]

In passages where Newman refers to an act of certitude 'after the proof' (329) he can be misleading. But it is clear that he does not intend a temporal progression — he clearly says that it is *not* that '*reason comes first,* and *then* comes the will and *faith.*'[47] The emphasis is on the *active* recognition of the sufficiency of the evidence. The recognition is part of the intellectual appraisal. Thus, what might appear to be a description of a choice or decision to effect certitude is an attempt to point out the active nature of a 'recognition'.

As noted in the Introduction, a number of philosophical discussions have pointed out the impossibility of *directly* creating belief by an act of will, a *fiat*. We have shown that Newman was not committed to such a position. What is interesting to note at this point is that such critiques of 'Cartesian volitionalism' sometimes swing the pendulum to another extreme — namely, that of belief as an automatic reaction. Louis Pojman, following Bernard Williams writes that 'belief as a judgement is not an act but a *happening*'.[48] Such assent is an 'automatic nod', 'involuntary' — 'once the objective factors are recognized, the assent comes automatically, of itself'.[49] In like manner, H. H. Price concludes that deciding that *p* is 'not a free choice at all, but a forced one'.[50] The implication is that the only alternatives are (1) a direct willing to believe (which is impossible), or (2) an auto-

---

[46] Cf. James's essay, 'The Will to Believe' in *The Will to Believe; Human Immortality* (New York: Dover Publ. Inc., 1956).

[47] 17 June 1846, in Pailin, *The Way to Faith,* Appendix III.

[48] 'Belief and Will', *Religious Studies* 14 (March 1978), p. 4.

[49] Ibid., p. 7.

[50] 'Belief and Will', *Proc. Aristotelian Society Supplement* 28 (1954), p. 16.

matic, involuntary reflex reaction in the face of 'objective' facts. The illegitimacy of such a dichotomy was, as we have seen, precisely what Newman was trying to call attention to; moreover, I suggest that his account of an 'active recognition' does more justice to the relation between belief and will than does the opposition of free choice to forced, involuntary reflex reactions.

For much the same reason, the denial that a choice is necessary to effect certitude does not mean that certitude is therefore a 'direct insight'.[51] Such an interpretation can easily fail to do justice to Newman's emphasis on the *active* appropriation involved. Talk about 'insight' and 'intuition' generally seems to misrepresent Newman's thought precisely in the direction of the 'passive impression made on the mind' which he strongly rejected.[52]

B. Deliberate Commitment: The Role of the Will AFTER Certitude is experienced

The role of the will in relation to certainty is not exhausted, however, by the personal contribution in the whole reasoning process. Since the believer can affirm or stifle the certainty he experiences, the will can play a role after certitude is reached. The repose and persistence we experience after examination of an assent are both a function of the assurance we naturally and directly feel. Since we can extinguish certainty as well as give it up out of moral weakness or intellectual instability, it is important to stress the need to affirm it. That is what Newman means by saying that full assent is not created and maintained solely by the reasoning faculty[53] — it is not created without the contribution of the 'whole person' and it is not maintained without our deliberate affirmation.

His claim that the 'state of mental certainty depends ultimately on the will', though it could refer to the first role of the will, is more likely to be a description of the second role since Newman explains it as follows:

In my *judgement* then the evidence is not simply demonstrative — but *certainty* is a state of mind, and in spite of this *judgement*, I suppose we

---

[51] For example, Fey's *Faith and Doubt*.
[52] Even though Newman himself sometimes uses the term.
[53] *T.P.*, p. 125 (20 July 1865).

are *certain* without any sort of fear of mistake, that the proposition in question is true. At the same time I think that the state of mental certainty depends ultimately on the will — and that the will could so act upon the mind as to lead it morbidly to make that microscopic objection an occasion of doubt.[54]

Newman stresses how we can, in a sort of intellectual neurosis, undermine the certainty we in fact feel. Affirmation of or commitment to the certainty we experience might also be necessary, as Newman sometimes implies, if the certitude requires a great deal from us. Moral and religious beliefs place demands on us; they 'cost' and it would be nice, we might sometimes think, if we were not so certain that they were true and therefore that we must act accordingly. In addition, moral and religious beliefs are often challenged by our peers, sometimes by peers whose intellectual capacities we marvel at, sometimes with arguments we feel unable to master.

Newman once asked whether it was possible to stifle certainty, 'conviction remaining'.[55] He concluded that it was possible by means of introducing doubts and attempting to undermine the experienced certitude. Striking confirmation of Newman's point is offered, ironically, in an article by his critic Leslie Stephen. Stephen writes that 'It is our duty to believe what appears to us to be proved'.[56] This is not a superfluous admonition, he claims, because 'the reason has to reckon with instincts as powerful as irrational'. He explains:

I may know that I am absolutely safe when I am at the brink of a precipice, but my body declines to be convinced, and shudders and turns giddy in spite of conclusive evidence. A demonstration may be as clear to me as a proposition of Euclid; but fear of authority, or dread of consequences, or mere blind sympathy with others, may prevent its real assimilation. To believe what we know to be certain at times even requires a kind of intellectual heroism.[57]

Whatever the source of the impulse, then, Newman knew that we could be moved to stifle our certitude. It was appropriate therefore to encourage a confirmation or commitment to the certitude we experience in the face of intellectual and moral weakness.

---

[54] *L.D.*, 18: 334 (letter to Haydon, 24 Apr. 1858). Emphasis Newman's.
[55] *T.P.*, p. 14 (13 May 1853).
[56] 'The Scepticism of Believers', in *An Agnostic's Apology*, p. 46.
[57] Ibid., p. 47.

But it must be remembered that Newman is here referring to willing as a consequence rather than a source of certainty. The choice to affirm the certitude is neither a source nor a substitute for certainty. Passages in which certainty seems related to choice therefore reveal, rather than obscure, the full extent of Newman's views on religious certitude by highlighting the relation of certitude to religious commitment as a whole. This second role of the will is a deliberate act of intending to adhere, in contrast to the non-deliberate or non-intentional adherence that is part of certitude itself.

Newman's distinction between two roles of the will thus indirectly highlights two different senses of religious commitment — a deliberate and a non-deliberate commitment — which we will consider in more detail in Chapters V and VI. This is an important contribution to the philosophy of religion, since it reveals a greater complexity in the question of the relation between doubt and religious commitment than has usually been recognized. The next chapter will begin the consideration of the persistence and resistance to change in belief which are involved in both the deliberate and non-deliberate commitments. In this way we can finally determine the implications concerning rational criticism in Newman's model of religious adherence.

CHAPTER

IV

A 'Grammar of Assent' which only vindicates Assent at the expense of reason, and secures Certitude by isolating it from the processes of thought out of which it comes, may make a foundation for credulity; it can never help us to render a reason for the Faith that is in us.

Review article, *Edinburgh Review*
October 1870

... if I understand Dr. Newman and his 'illative sense', the sort of foundation on which religious belief should stand is this:— look out a few topics which as they stand render your creed probable, and then by the help of your 'illative sense' get a certitude of its truth before you have had time to consider any facts which look in the other direction.

Fitzjames Stephen, 'On Certitude in Religious Assent', *Frazer's Magazine*
January 1872

We have considered Newman's view of certitude in terms of its active, uncompelled though constrained character. The focus has been on Newman's understanding of the generation of the assurance involved. Certitude is characterized not only by assurance, however, but also by 'persistence': certitude is a complex act in which 'keenness in believing is united with repose and persistence' (216). This element of persistence is crucial to genuine religious devotion:

Without certitude in religious faith there may be much decency of profession and of observance, but there can be no habit of prayer, no directness of devotion, no intercourse with the unseen, no generosity of self-sacrifice. Certitude then is essential to the Christian; and if he is to persevere to the end, his certitude must include in it a principle of persistence. (220)

The idea of a 'principle of persistence' which allows an individual to 'persevere to the end' has seemed to some modern critics of Christianity to be a strategy for attempting to legitimate the wilful suppression of doubt in the face of counter-evidence. William Bartley III, for example, strikingly developed this objection to early twentieth-century Protestant neo-orthodoxy.[1] Bartley deplored the appeal he saw in neo-orthodoxy to 'absolute presuppositions' which were not only unjustifiable but also uncriticizable. Rationality, according to Bartley, consists of criticizability of beliefs, yet Christianity prohibits criticism of its beliefs by its adherents. 'Theologians', Bartley claimed, 'have argued that not only to abandon allegiance to Christianity, but even to subject that allegiance to criticism is to forsake Christianity.'[2] The Christian, unlike Bartley's comprehensively critical rationalist, cannot 'consider and be moved by criticism' of his commitment.[3] Barth's idea that faith is a 'decision *once for all*' represented for Bartley the supreme example of irrational insulation of beliefs from criticism.[4]

Although certain aspects of Bartley's theory of rationality are problematical,[5] I agree that rendering our beliefs immune to criticism, by fiat, once for all, is an intellectually indefensible position. A number of Newman's contemporary critics, however, saw him as prescribing just such a position; Newman's *Grammar* was made the particular target of the widespread charge that Roman Catholicism's prescriptions enslaved the intellects of its followers.[6] Then, as now, it seemed to some that Newman was simply throwing reason to the winds.[7]

At first glance a number of Newman's key claims seem to provide considerable warrant for the charges of his critics.

---

[1] *Retreat to Commitment* (New York: Alfred A. Knopf, 1962).
[2] Ibid., p. 150. [3] Ibid., p. 172.
[4] Ibid., p. 172. The reference is to Barth's *Dogmatics in Outline* (New York: Harper Torchbooks, 1959), p. 20.
[5] Cf. William Austin, 'Religious Commitment and the Logical Status of Doctrines', *Religious Studies* 9 (Mar. 1973); W. D. Hudson, 'Professor Bartley's Theory of Rationality and Religious Commitment', *Religious Studies* 9 (Sept. 1973); Martin Marty, 'Religious Commitment and Rational Criticism', *Philosophical Forum* 2 (Fall 1970). [6] Ward II, pp. 271–2.
[7] Cf. 'Dr. Newman's *Grammar of Assent*', *The Edinburgh Review* 132 (Apr. 1870) for a vehement charge of irrationality; also cf. B. M. G. Reardon's *Religious Thought in the Nineteenth Century* (Cambridge: Cambridge University Press, 1966), p. 272.

For example, Newman claims that assent is *independent* of inference and that assent is *incompatible with doubt*. In addition, he claims that certitude is indefectible and that we can legitimately make a 'promise' never to change. The following two chapters will discuss certitude and the promise that religious commitment involves. In this chapter I shall consider the first set of claims — the independence of assent from inference, and the incompatibility of assent and doubt — and examine their implications for the question of the criticizability of assents. I shall be arguing that the significance of the claim to independence lies in its reference to a particular *mode* of adherence to and abandonment of assent, and that the incompatibility of doubt prescribed by Newman does not entail immunity to criticism. Both these conclusions will be relevant to the question of the criticizability of certitude and the defeasibility of religious commitment as a whole.

1. The Independence of Assent

What do Newman's claims about the independence of assent tell us about the kind of doubt Newman saw as incompatible with assent? Does independence mean, as critics then suggested, that Newman was isolating assent from rational processes; does independence imply that assent is rendered immune to criticism? An affirmative answer would mean that certitude is *a fortiori* rendered immune to criticism. In order to determine the implications of the proposed independence I shall examine the separability of assent and inference, the rational justification of assent, and the possibility of reversal of assent.

A. Independence and Separability

Inference, as noted earlier, is conditional because it is dependent on its premises:

An act of Inference includes in its object the dependence of its thesis upon its premises, that is, upon a relation, which is an abstraction; but an act of Assent rests wholly on the thesis as its object. (40)

Assent, therefore, cannot be dependent on premises in the same way as inference is dependent. Inference, moreover, is 'ever varying in strength' (38); assent, if unconditional, cannot merely reflect the variation of strength in inference. In discussing one variety of assent, the notional assent called 'opinion', Newman claims that opinion and inference are distinct acts of the mind because although the inferential conclusion varies in strength with the reasoning involved, 'opinion, as being an assent, is independent of premisses' (59). What sort of independence is Newman proposing here?

Newman's manner of illustrating independence in this particular case is ambiguous, since he immediately goes on to say:

we have opinions which we never think of defending by argument, though, of course, we think they can be so defended. We are even obstinate in them . . . and may say that we have a right to think just as we please, reason or no reason; whereas Inference is in its nature and by its profession conditional and uncertain. (59)

This independence of opinions from premisses proposed here can be considered in two ways: (1) in the case where opinions are held 'reason or no reason', or (2) where opinions are maintained without recourse to reasons 'though, of course, we think they can be so defended'. In what follows I want to suggest that Newman's understanding of the normative relation between assent and inference is not to be determined solely by reference to his examples of their separability. In effect I shall be showing that Newman's view of the independence of assent is not to be understood along the lines of the first option, 'reason, or no reason'.

The spadework Newman saw as necessary in order to rebut the 'pretentious axiom' that probable reasons can never lead to certainty (160) consisted in showing that assent and inference are in fact distinct acts. Newman begins his task of showing that assent is a substantive act, separable from inference, with a catalogue of the marks which will signal the achievement of that task. Assent will have been shown to be a distinct and substantive act

if in matter of fact they are not always found together, — if they do not vary with each other, — . . . if one is strong when the other is weak, — if sometimes they seem even in conflict with each other. (166)

Thus, Newman sets out in the section on 'Simple Assent' to find out what is the case about the relation of assent and inference 'in matter of fact'.

Newman's descriptions of the 'matter of fact' about the relation between assent and inference fall into two categories. In one case we *once* had justifying inference even though we are no longer conscious of it: 'Assents may endure without the presence of the inferential acts upon which they were originally elicited' (167). In the other case we fail to assent or to maintain assent even when the reasons are recognized as good. This can be due to moral causes, 'arising out of our condition, age, company, occupations, fortunes', etc. (168). 'Prejudice' and 'moral motives' can hinder assent to 'incontrovertible proofs' and conclusions which are 'logically unimpeachable' (169). Sometimes admittedly good arguments do not incline our minds to assent at all; anything less than a 'short and lucid' mathematical demonstration can suffer interference in the promptness of our assent (170).[8]

What Newman succeeds in showing in these cases is that assent and inference are separable. In particular he shows that (A) our inference is neither a sufficient cause nor a psychologically necessary sustaining condition of assent, and (B) that assent is not always as a 'matter of fact' exactly proportioned to inference. In these examples Newman has achieved what he seems to have set out to achieve — namely, a descriptive task. The independence of assent here is like the independence of appropriate action from belief: 'as . . . men may believe without practising, so is assent also independent of our acts of inference' (169).

B. Rational Justification

If the examples about the 'matter of fact' which Newman gave were intended to be normative prescriptions rather than descriptions Newman would, in addition to going beyond the limits of his stated intention, also be contradicting explicit claims he makes elsewhere concerning the need for rational justification of assents. Prejudice is, after all, recognized by him to be irrational (258); the fact that he recognizes that it does in fact hinder assent is scarcely reason for suggesting that he thinks it *rightly* can. Though in his examples he says that admittedly good arguments do not incline the mind to assent at all, he admits elsewhere that they should (171) even

[8] Cf. Ward II, p. 248 (letter to Wilberforce, 1868).

though our assent when it comes is total. Moreover, if the conclusion that we *can* refuse to assent to conclusions which are logically unimpeachable is read as sanctioning such actions, it conflicts with Newman's claim elsewhere that if we refuse to assent in such a case we 'act against our nature' (229).

More general evidence of Newman's position on the need for rational justification is found in his strong emphasis on inference as a *sine qua non* condition of assent (13, 41). Although not an adequate condition, it is necessary, even if only implicit. The importance of rational justification is something he thinks he has belaboured so much that he 'surely . . . need not enlarge' on it (157). Assent cannot be given 'rightly' without sufficient grounds (171). Sometimes our assent must go further then the analysable evidence warrants, but there must be adequate grounds for whatever side we opt; we must have *'reason enough* to resolve to place faith'.[9] It would be wrong, he says, for a person to become a Catholic 'without his *judgement* being convinced', though of course people may have 'very good reasons which they cannot bring together into words'.[10]

Newman's requirement that Faith be 'approvable' by Reason, announced in his *University Sermons*,[11] was repeated in 1860 when he wrote the following:

I grant then that, as soon as a person can use his reason, and so far forth as he exercises it, he ought to exercise it on religion, and should place his faith upon it as an antecedent condition in the order of nature.[12]

This position is articulated in a letter to Froude written in 1879:

You seem to think that I hold that in religion the will is simply to supersede the intellect, and that we are to force ourselves to believe against evidence, or at least in some way or other not give the mind fair play in the question of accepting or rejecting Christianity. I will say then what I really mean . . . I hold most distinctly that, tho' faith is the result of the will, itself ever follows intellectual judgement.[13]

In addition to these explicit theoretical expressions, we find warrant in Newman's own life. His whole account in the *Apologia Pro Vita Sua* testifies to his view of the necessity of

---

[9] Harper, p. 91 (20 Oct. 1851).   [10] Ibid., p. 99 (10 Apr. 1854).
[11] *U.S.*, pp. 182–3.   [12] *T.P.*, p. 86 (12 Jan. 1860).
[13] Harper, p. 208 (29 Apr. 1879).

rational grounds — there he saw his situation as one in which reason must overcome affection.[14] Newman's semi-auto-biographical novel, *Loss and Gain: The Story of a Convert,* reinforces this conclusion; for example, he has Charles Reding say: 'Surely God wills us to be guided by reason . . . surely we ought not to act without it, against it.'[15]

If there is a tension in Newman's thought on the idea of rational justification it could be attributed to the need Newman felt to argue against many of the assumptions of the rationalism informing Liberalism, while doing justice to the importance and necessity of rational justification.[16] But, on the whole, the emphasis on rational justification seems abundantly clear and provides significant evidence against the argument that Newman finds reason either 'useless' or 'dangerous' in religion.[17]

Newman has attempted to show that assent may be 'withheld in cases when there are good reasons for giving it to a proposition', or 'withdrawn after it has been given, the reasons remaining', or 'remain when the reasons are forgotten' as well as that assent need not 'vary in strength as the reasons vary' (172). All of this, he says, establishes the point that he has wanted to make — the point that assent is a 'substantive' act, 'distinct' from inference. Since he clearly states at the same time that the distinction he has shown does not mean that there is no 'legitimate or actual connection' between assent and inference or that assent can be 'rightly given without sufficient grounds' (171) it does seem that he has intended to show only separability up to this point. When understood as

[14] *Apo.* pp. 57–9, 112, 172.

[15] 6th ed. (London: Burns, Oates & Co., 1874), p. 210. Also see pp. 43, 142, 314.

[16] Cf. Edward Sillem's discussion of 'Liberalism', *The Philosophical Notebook of John Henry Newman,* Vol. 1: General Introduction to the Study of Newman's Philosophy (Louvain: Nauwelaerts Publ., 1969), pp. 30–66. Also cf. A. J. Boekraad, *The Personal Conquest of Truth,* pp. 46–9, 159–60.

[17] Jay Newman, 'Cardinal Newman's Phenomenology of Religious Belief', suggests that 'in Chapter 4 of the *Grammar,* Newman seems to be arguing that reason in religion is at best useless and at worst dangerous' although he (Newman) later is forced to make 'concessions to reason', p. 133. His conclusion is that Newman's view of notional assent implies a rejection of 'all rational approaches to religious belief', p. 133. Newman, however, clearly admits the value of notional assents — cf. Chap. I, n. 6.

description attempting to show the distinctness of assent, Newman's discussion is consistent with both his explicit claims concerning his project and his claims concerning the necessity of rational justification.

It is interesting to note that even if these descriptions were attempts to legitimate the refusal to assent to *p* when there are good reasons for assent to *p,* this would not necessarily mean that Newman approved acting against what our reasoning leads to. First, there might conceivably be good justifying reasons on both sides,[18] in which case we are not being authorized to assent to not-*p* without good grounds. Secondly, we might find it intellectually responsible to suspend our judgement, in which case we are not being authorized to assent to not-*p* without good grounds either. A normative claim that we can withhold assent to *p* even when there are good grounds for *p* does not *in itself,* there-fore, urge a blind commitment in reverse. If such a normative claim, however, were to be consistent with claims about the need for rational justification, it would have to be under-stood along these lines. If inference is a *sine qua non* con-dition of assent to *p,* it must equally be a *sine qua non* condition of assent to not-*p.* Newman, himself, notes that we cannot use reason 'by halves'.[19] If we act against our nature (as he says we do) in refusing to assent to *p* when the argu-met approaches the limit of proof (229), then we likewise act against our nature when we refuse to assent to not-*p* in similar conditions. That Newman would agree seems clear from his assertion that our intellectual nature is under laws to seal up the conclusions to which ratiocination brings us (229).

Having seen Newman's *sine qua non* requirement of infer-ence and his general emphasis on rational justification, we are led to ask how this relates to the independence of assent from inference. Does that independence mean that we can legitimately hold on 'no matter what' to any assent as long as that assent is initially reached by way of inference? Can we hold on 'come way may'? Does a later variation in the

---

[18] Andrew Zvara, 'On Claiming to Know and Feeling Sure', *Philosophical Studies* 24 (July 1973), pp. 273–4; cf. also Adam Morton, 'Our Knowledge of Theory', unpublished MS, Chap. I.   [19] *Idea,* p. 358.

inference have no necessary effect on our assent; does it require no change on our part? Is the assent allowed to be permanently and totally immune to criticism once reached on rational grounds. In sum, what are the implications of the independence of assent?

C. Reversibility

The significance of the independence of assent can be derived in part from some comments Newman made in an 1848 paper on the nature and cause of faith. Here Newman writes that 'assent does not really depend on those motiva [reasons], for no conclusion can be more certain than the premises from which it is drawn. In other words, *it is not resolvable into its motiva*'.[20] The claim concerning the independence of assent is intended, therefore, to emphasize this lack of exhaustive reducibility. That it is not resolvable into the inference, however, does not require that the assent be immune to variations in those reasons.

A far more important indication of what independence entails is given in Newman's clear admission that investigations of our simple assents 'whether in religious subjects or secular, often issue in the reversal of the assents which they were originally intended to confirm' (192). Just as arguments embolden and protect our assents (186), by the same token they can finally tell against them:

if, as time goes on, [our assents] give way, our change of mind, be it for good or for evil, is owing to the accumulating force of the arguments, sound or unsound, which bear down upon the propositions which we have hitherto received. (194)

Reversal can be warranted, therefore ('for good' as well as 'for evil') and based on the force of objections. The effect of objections, however, is *indirect*:

Objections indeed, as such, have no direct force to weaken assent; but, when they multiply, they tell against the implicit reasonings or the formal inferences which are its warrant, and suspend its acts and gradually undermine its habit. (194)

In the process of investigating our assents, we can come to discover objections which converge, multiply, and lead us to

---

[20] Paper on the 'Nature and Cause of Faith', 1848, cited by Pailin, *The Way to Faith*, Appendix III, p. 208, emphasis mine.

suspend our acts of assent. However, the assent itself is not gradually weakened — there are no degrees of assent. We do not hold the proposition with more hesitation or more reserve in the face of mounting objections, yet we can eventually abandon it altogether.

The illustration Newman provides is that of a student who has difficulty in making his answer tally with the answer in his textbook. Newman asks 'Does his trust in it fall down a certain number of degrees, according to the force of his difficulty?' (180) On the contrary, in spite of the difficulty, he remains 'unshaken' in his adherence to the book's conclusion. He holds it without reserve, 'faithful to his belief in [the book's] correctness, till its incorrectness is actually proved' (180). The implication is that it *can* be proved incorrect; we can know that, however, and still hold on without hesitation until it is proven incorrect, since we neither expect nor suspect that it will be proven incorrect. Newman correctly notes that 'to incur a risk is not to expect reverse' (193). The denial of change in a particular manner (namely, the weakening of our unconditional acceptance by degrees) is not an all-out denial of the possibility of any change. We can finally reverse our assent, but we should do so only after maintaining a particular kind of adherence in the meantime.

The independence of assent from inference does not preclude the recognition that an abandonment of our assent may be warranted. It does mean, however, that our assent does not vary *directly* with the ups and downs of the inferential warrants. In this respect Newman's normative understanding is closely related to his descriptive claim noted earlier that assent need not vary '*as* the reasons vary'. But the claim is normative only when understood in terms of a *manner* of adherence. Changes in the inferential warrants do affect our assents, and rightly so — but only in a particular manner. That is, objections do not make us more and more tentative, weakening our assent little by little. They do not lead to piecemeal abandonment of unconditional acceptance, or to an increasingly conditional acceptance. But they can overwhelm us. Converging probabilities inclined us to assent to *p,* even though the assent when it came was total. So too, converging probabilities can incline us to assent to not-*p,* but

our assent to that, when it comes, along with our abandonment of *p,* is likewise total. In the meantime our assent
remains unconditional. It is in this sense that assent is
independent of inference; therefore, the independence of
assent does not prejudice the rationality of assent.

Newman's support for the legitimacy of such independence
can be found in his many references to the complexity of
implicit reasoning and the consequent difficulty of analysing
'a proof satisfactorily, the result of which good sense actually
guarantees to us' (296). If there is a cumulative case, a mass
of converging probabilities which lead to an assent, objections
to any individual probabilities need not undermine the whole
complex. Moreover, because of the difficulty of adequately
analysing our warrants, the reasons we produce may often be
unsatisfactory (303). He graphically elaborates his claim that
men often 'see the truth, but they do not know how they see
it' as follows:

if at any time they attempt to prove it, it is as much a matter of experiment with them, as if they had to find a road to a distant mountain,
which they see with the eye; and they get entangled, embarrassed, and
perchance overthrown in the superfluous endeavour. (380)

Newman here illustrates the case of a person who experiences
X and then attempts to justify it, and does so poorly. In such
case objections to the justification do not *directly* affect the
assent — the person may try to establish another better
justification — though they may ultimately affect it. One can
also extrapolate from this to the case of a person who as a
result of a cumulative argument comes to a belief which
allows him to experience X. He then has reason to consider
objections to his initial warrants as unable to affect his
assent directly, even though he cannot immediately justify
his assent in a more satisfactory way. The process of not
letting counter-evidence weaken assent by degrees is not
equivalent to a process of continually refusing to let evidence
affect assent at all.

Another way in which change of assents could be understood while maintaining the independence of assent from
inference is in terms of the possibility of assenting to variations in strength of inference. Newman admitted that we
could unconditionally accept a probability, for example (175).

Assent is all or nothing; change of assent is all or nothing — but we can totally accept varying inferences. It is probably for this reason that Newman could write, as late as the *Apologia,* about a 'graduated scale of assent'.[21] It is also for this reason that the denial of degrees of assent does not entail the disastrous consequence of allowing assents concerning *p* only when the evidence for *p* is overwhelming, as some critics have suggested.[22] Still another way in which Newman seems to allow for change is seen in his concession that although assent cannot change by degrees, the *habit* of assent to *p* can be gradually undermined (194). Apparently we can refuse to assent occasionally, while not assenting less each time we do assent, until the habit goes — and it is the formation of the habit that is crucial to religion (184).

The crucial thing to remember is that Newman's admission that reversal of assents can be warranted precludes the independence of assent from legitimating a dogmatic refusal never to change our assent or a dogmatic adherence to our initial assent *no matter what.* I shall argue later that this conclusion is relevant also to certitudes or reflex assents.

2. The 'Dubitability' of Assent

In principle, then, the independence of assent from inference does not mean that assent is rendered immune to criticism, nor does it mean that we cannot recognize that critical investigation may prove fatal to some of our assents. But if Newman admits that our assents can be rightly overturned, and that we can recognize this ahead of time, how can he say that doubt is incompatible with assent, as he does?[23] Can he say consistently both that 'Assent indeed to a professed truth and doubt of it are incompatible'[24] and that the reversal of assents can be warranted?

As a preliminary to the more important consideration of

---

[21] *Apo.,* p. 31.
[22] H. H. Price, for example, seems to assume that such a consequence ensues — see *Belief,* Lecture 6, esp. pp. 155–6. I. T. Ker, 'Recent Critics of Newman's *Grammar*', *Religious Studies* 13 (Mar. 1977) provides what I consider a good critique of Price's objections to Newman.
[23] *G.A.,* p. 6.   [24] *T.P.,* p. 131 (17 Apr. 1866).

the relation between doubt and religious certitude, I will here examine (1) what kind of doubt Newman sees as incompatible with assent, and (2) what kind of 'dubitability', if any, is implicit in the possibility of warranted reversal of assents. If we decide later that there is something peculiar to certitude which renders criticism of it either descriptively or normatively impossible, these conclusions about assent will at least be of value in explicating more clearly Newman's views on doubt and assent. If, on the contrary, a plausible case can be made for criticizability of certitudes, these conclusions might well contribute to our understanding of the relation between doubt and certitudes.

It should be noted first of all that Newman offers several general definitions of 'doubt': in the *Grammar* 'doubt' is defined as 'suspense of mind' (7); in the Roman Catholic emendations of the *Via Media* he defines it as a 'withholding of assent'.[25] According to such definitions the incompatibility of doubt and assent is a logical and trivial matter — we cannot do X and not-X at the same time. Our inquiry regains its importance, however, as soon as we realize that we still need to determine what for Newman constitutes suspension or withholding of assent. The discovery made earlier that according to Newman we can rightly reverse our assents, or that we can realize that such a reversal may be warranted, makes clear that Newman's prohibition on doubt does not imply a prohibition on all processes or attitudes which might eventually lead to suspense of assent. Thus, while assents are by definition incapable of coexisting with doubt (they are mutually exclusive modes of holding propositions), the proposition assented to is not indubit*able* in an absolute sense. Some kind of dubitability of the proposition seems to be a necessary condition of the criticizability Newman allows. But the dubitability must have limits; it cannot allow what would constitute the withholding of assent.

The attempt to determine what Newman rules out by the unconditionality and independence of assent as well as what is left as the basis of criticizability should begin with another look at Newman's description of the process of reviewing

[25] See Note 4, p. 85.

simple assents. In the example noted earlier of the mathematical conclusion that did not tally with the book, Newman concluded that although we 'incur a risk' we do not 'expect reverse'. Such investigation is legitimate in all cases of simple assent:

We do not deny our own faith, because we become controversialists; and in like manner we may employ ourselves in proving what we already believe to be true, simply in order to ascertain the producible evidence in its favour, and in order to fulfill what is due to ourselves and to the claims and responsibilities of our education and social position. (190-1)

Investigation not only can be, but *is,* a duty for educated people (192). Such investigation, however, is to be clearly distinguished, according to Newman, from another process of reasoning which is condemned — namely, the process of 'inquiry'. Investigation is the examination of the grounds for the truth of p; it does not involve a suspension of assent to p while the investigation is being conducted. Inquiry, on the other hand, as Newman uses the term, refers to a process initiated by suspension of assent. When assent is suspended (and, also, presumably when we initially have no assent to p or not-p) we are in a condition of doubt. In inquiring, then, we are in doubt where the truth lies; in the process of investigating we are merely attempting to justify p. Investigation is therefore compatible with assent, while inquiry is not.

According to this explication of investigation and inquiry the difference between the two seems to lie in the *mode of approach*. The inquiry that is ruled incompatible with assent is the dropping of a given assent in order to determine its truth or falsity. Newman gives our assents a presumption in their favour. We must hold on to them without hesitancy while we attempt to determine and lay out their grounds. The difference between investigation and inquiry, therefore, does not refer to the content of the propositions concerned. Apparently *any* proposition can be investigated.

Part of Newman's explanation for the claim that inquiry is 'inconsistent' with assent, however, raises a question about whether the content or significance of the proposition might be a relevant consideration. Newman suggests that inquiry places us 'outside of the Church' (191). That is, it is inconsistent with 'retain[ing] the name of believer'; such 'doubting excludes believing' — it is already 'lost faith' (191). Such an illustration of the meaning of inquiry suggests a distinction which has been important to a number of 'fideists' who stress the difference between the questioning of ground-rule assumptions of the religious system and the internal criticism of things within the system. Such a distinction is not limited to those fideists influenced by Wittgenstein. Karl Barth uses the same distinction, arguing that doubt about presuppositions of Christian theism is contrary to faith, but criticism and doubt within the system (though a little dangerous) is part of the enterprise of theology.[26] There are, however, important differences between Newman's approach and fideistic approaches. The most fundamental difference concerns the relevance of rational justification for Newman. In addition to the points raised in the discussion of the importance of rational justification in section 1B, we can point to Newman's admission of a natural theology as well as to concessions like the following:

Few minds in earnest can remain at ease without some sort of rational grounds for their religious belief; to reconcile theory and fact is almost an instinct of the mind. When then a flood of facts [from natural science], ascertained or suspected, comes pouring in upon us, with a multitude of others in prospect, all believers in Revelation, be they Catholic or not, are roused to consider their bearing upon themselves. . . . It would ill become me, as if I were afraid of truth of any kind, . . . to be angry with science, because religion is bound in duty to take cognizance of its teaching.[27]

Finally, Newman also allows that inquiry is able to get us back into the circle of believers (191).

At least in part Newman's understanding of the doubt that is incompatible with assent concerns doubt which puts us outside the circle of believers. But since he seems to make any assent in principle open to investigation, we can conclude that the distinction between inquiry and investigation refers for Newman to different attitudes or modes of approach to any proposition rather than to different categories of propositions. It should be noted in passing that the concepts of 'investigation' and 'inquiry', even as Newman defines them, are more closely related than he may have realized. A process

---

[26] See Introduction, nn. 14 and 15.
[27] Cf. *Apo.*, p. 31, and *G.A.*, pp. 98, 100, 389–408; *Apo.*, pp. 233–4.

of investigation of p will involve the suspension of assents to certain propositions which we are considering as possible evidence for p. The legitimation of investigation thus seems to imply the legitimation of some inquiry as well — though of course investigation of p does not require inquiring about p.

In sum, the doubt that is descriptively incompatible with assent — the doubt that cannot coexist with assent — is suspense of assent. The doubt that is ruled out prescriptively by Newman is the dropping of an assent in order to see where the truth lies. Assents, or more precisely those propositions to which we assent are not for that reason indubitable. Some kind of dubitability is implied in the criticizability or corrigibility of these assents. Our task now is to specify more precisely the character, extent and limits of that dubitability.

In his description of investigation Newman refers to the 'vague consciousness of the possibility of a reversal' (193). This suggests one way to assess the dubitability of assents — namely, by an analysis of the 'possibility' we recognize. Newman points to the dubitability which he considers legitimate and compatible with assent in his discussion of that 'class of writers' who 'have themselves as little misgiving about the truths which they pretend to weigh out and measure, as their unsophisticated neighbours' yet who 'think it a duty to remind us, that since the full etiquette of logical requirements has not been satisfied, we must believe those truths at our peril' (181). His judgement is that they were simply warning us 'that an issue which can never come to pass in matter of fact, is nevertheless in theory a possible supposition' (181). I suggest that two different interpretations of this passage are possible, with different implications for Newman's understanding of doubt and criticizability.

First, the 'in theory possible supposition' could refer to a category of propositions which are *logically* possible. That is, not-p is 'in theory a possible supposition' because p is not logically entailed by its premises. Here Newman would be recognizing that all concrete conclusions are *logically* dubitable. Moreover, Newman claims that even when not-p is logically possible (i.e. even when p is logically dubitable) there are times when not-p can 'never come to pass in matter of fact'. Here Newman would be rightly arguing against the sceptic that mere logical dubitability is not a ground for reasonable doubt.

If Newman is referring in this passage to *logical* dubitability, however, his formulation suggests that the contrast between 'in theory' possible and 'in matter of fact' possible parallels a contrast between logically possible and more-than-logically possible. Since Newman's intent is clearly to argue that something may not be reasonable ground for doubt even if it is 'in theory' possible, the implicit obverse in this case is the concession that what *can* 'come to pass in matter of fact' (*ex hypothesi*, what is more-than-logically possible) *is* ground for reasonable doubt and precludes an unconditional acceptance. On such a reading Newman would be equating ground for reasonable doubt of *p* with the more-than-logical possibility of not-*p*. He would be committing himself to the claim that the admission that not-*p* is more-than-logically possible is incompatible with assent. We can assent only when the doubt we recognize is not more than that involved in the admission that the negation is not logically contradictory. Newman's reference to the 'full etiquette of logical requirements' supports this reading of what constitutes the legitimate dubitability of assents.

A second reading of the passage, however, is possible according to which Newman would not be committed to the claim that it is reasonable to doubt all more-than-logically dubitable conclusions. The example he uses in the passage is that Great Britain is an island. This example — like the whole list of examples on pages 177–8 — suggests at first glance that he was not concerned with *logical* dubitability at all. It suggests that he was not merely talking about the doubt that is possible because the negation of our beliefs is not logically contradictory. Moreover, his claim that in investigating assents our minds are 'not moved by a scientific computation of chance, nor can any law of averages affect my particular case' (193) suggests that he was not merely talking about logical dubitability. Both things suggest that he could have believed that not all grounds for the falsehood of a belief are reasonable, even if they are more-than-logically possible. On such a reading Newman would have been suggesting a more informed and informative distinction than the traditional one

between logical dubitability and more-than-logical dubitability. The 'in theory possible supposition' he would be
referring to, in this case, is one that is possible for more
reasons than that it is not logically contradictory. Not-p is
'really' possible — possible without changing the constitution
of the world as we know it — yet it cannot 'come to pass in
matter of fact' in a given case. Thus, more-than-logical
dubitability does not necessarily provide reasonable grounds
for doubt.

Both Newman's critique of the relevance of logic to real
life, and his understanding of the relation between normative
and empirical judgements lend support to a claim that, in his
distinction between theoretically possible supposition and
what is none the less not possible 'in matter of fact', Newman
was assuming that what is 'in theory a possible supposition'
cannot be determined solely by reference to *logical* properties.
I suggested earlier that Newman's judgements about the
relation of right reasoning and empirical judgements could be
illuminated by reference to the way Wittgenstein, Quine and
others later saw the judgements of 'necessary' or 'certain'
truths to be a result of our 'determination' to channel our
experience in certain ways.[28] If I am correct in suggesting
that Newman's rejection of an *a priori* normative inquiry
implied an acceptance of the objectivity of determinations
bound by socially shared and 'relatively uniform' responses
to self and environment (for Newman, this meant a human
nature given and guaranteed by God), then the idea that
there is no fixed category of propositions which possess the
quality of 'logical indubitability' independently of human
judgement would not have been unacceptable to him. And if
'logical indubitability', a property of statements whose negation is necessarily contradictory, is effectively   an idle
category, then the category of 'logical dubitability' loses its
force too.

It is interesting to note in this respect a surprisingly
modern-sounding comment made by Newman on reading
Kant. He writes:

I am disposed to question whether such a distinction between necessary

---

[28] See Chap. III, pp. 66–70.

truth and induction or ⟨?⟩ empirical truth is possible in fact, though Kant makes it the starting point of his treatise.[29]

This resembles Wittgenstein's position that what is 'logically' unassailable is on a continuum with what is empirically unassailable. In a commentary on Wittgenstein, P. M. S. Hacker explains this as follows:

> The notion of the logically possible ... is now bound to a grammar. What is logically possible or impossible is wholly dependent upon what our grammar permits, what makes sense in a given language system (*PI* 520).... [The conventions that constitute grammar] are the only correlate in language to intrinsic necessities (*PI* 372). Essences are reflections of forms of representation, marks of concepts, and thus made rather than found. We create our forms of representation, prompted by our biological and psychological character, prodded by Nature, restrained by society and urged by our drive to master the world.[30]

Thus, for Wittgenstein, 'what-cannot-be-denied-without-logical-contradiction' is not a metaphysical entity waiting to be discovered; it is determined by the concrete functioning of a human community.

It should be repeated that for Newman the human community or language-game referred to could be nothing less than the entire human community with the constitution given it by God.[31] Given the qualifications noted earlier, Newman's defence of certainty and his attack on scepticism bear striking similarities to Wittgenstein's, once it is clear that Wittgenstein's fundamental concepts and distinctions need not be understood 'fideistically' or relativistically.[32] Wittgenstein's language-game discussions can and often do refer to the human language-game as such — for example, the way of life that uses material object language. Moreover, Wittgenstein's distinction between infallibility and the impossibility of mistake allow for the kind of objective truth that might be thought necessary for a theist.[33] None of this necessitates the use of Wittgensteinian categories to explicate Newman's claims, but I suggest that it legitimates that use

---

[29] *T.P.*, p. 65 (1860?, 'Assent and Intuition', Introduction). Arrow bracket indicates Newman's own addition. Fey, *Faith and Doubt*, p. 106, notes this same passage but has a differing conclusion.
[30] Hacker, *Insight and Illusion*, p. 181; cf. *On Certainty* §§ 454, 319.
[31] See Chap. III, p. 70.   [32] See Chap. III, n. 32.
[33] *On Certainty* §§ 554, 663; cf. *U.S.*, XV, p. 340.

where it seems to illuminate Newman's points.

For Wittgenstein the awareness of the character of human language and the relation between language and functioning led to a number of claims. First, he saw the corrigibility and dubitability of all human beliefs. This admission of fallibility was clearly shared by Newman (224).[34] This meta-level admission did not imply a genuine dubitability for either Wittgenstein or Newman. Both in his early and late writings Newman condemned the idea that we have a 'duty to doubt of everything'.[35] We need a reason to doubt; we only doubt *within* a system (377). Newman thus set forth quite clearly what C. S. Peirce, Wittgenstein, and others would later maintain — namely, universal doubt is unreasonable since we need grounds for doubting.[36] In contrast to the meta-admission of the dubitability of all human beliefs, genuine dubitability is an admission based on more than the abstract possibility of error which cannot be eliminated from human thought and action. Genuine dubitability is something for which there is a possibility of reasons one way or the other. Of itself, however, the admission of genuine dubitability does not tell us anything about what is reasonable or unreasonable to doubt in a given case. Wittgenstein points this out in *On Certainty* — 'What I need to shew is that a doubt is not necessary even when it is possible.'[37] Is not this what Newman meant by saying that doubt is often 'possible, but it must not be assumed', since 'to be just able to doubt is no warrant for disbelieving'.[38]

Wittgenstein elaborates his point in the *Investigations*:

But that is not to say that we are in doubt because it is possible for us to *imagine* a doubt. I can easily imagine someone always doubting before he opened his front door whether an abyss did not yawn behind it, and making sure about it before he went through the door (and he might on some occasion prove to be right) — but that does not make me doubt in the same case.[39]

[34] At least in his later writings; cf., however, *Dev.*, pp. 169-70.

[35] *G.A.*, p. 377; cf. *V.M. I*, pp. 2 and 138.

[36] *On Certainty* § § 114, 115, 160, 343, 354, 519, 652; cf. *Charles S. Peirce: Selected Writings*, pp. 40, 188, 189.

[37] *On Certainty* § 392. Thomas Morawetz's study of *On Certainty (Wittgenstein and Knowledge)* was unavailable before my manuscript was completed; however, Chap. 5 ('On Unreasonable and Impossible Doubt') is a suggestive complement to my own conclusions.   [38] *Dev.*, p. 71.   [39] No. 84.

That we can 'imagine' not-*p* and that someone might be 'right' about it show that Wittgenstein was talking about what is more-than-logically possible.

He illustrates the claim that when the 'logically' possible and impossible are on a continuum with the empirically possible and impossible, the contrast between what is reasonable to doubt or unreasonable to doubt does not line up with the contrast between logical and more-than-logical. However difficult it may be to draw the line between reasonable and unreasonable doubt, it is clear that for Wittgenstein doubt may be more-than-logically possible yet still be unreasonable. Not all genuine dubitability should operate as doubt in our reasonings.

I have been suggesting throughout that both Newman's examples and his understanding of the relation between normative and empirical judgements lend plausibility to a claim that his discussion of the 'in theory possible' supposition of not-*p* which generates the dubitability of *p* can best be understood in light of a Wittgensteinian claim that not all genuine dubitability is ground for reasonable doubt. According to this second interpretation not all more-than-logical dubitability is reasonable. Hence the dubitability or 'doubt' that is compatible with assent includes the recognition that *p* is genuinely dubitable, but that in this particular case it is unreasonable to doubt it. According to the first interpretation discussed, Newman would be claiming that the only doubt that is compatible with assent is the recognition of logical dubitability. The admission that not-*p* was more-than-logically possible would preclude assent to *p*. The two proposed interpretations differ, therefore, on what constitute reasonable grounds for doubt. Which interpretation is to be preferred depends on two things: which accounts best for the possibility of warranted reversal of assent, and which accounts best for the unconditionality of simple assent.

Although they differ concerning what constitutes reasonable grounds for doubt (i.e. for withholding assent), both interpretations agree on the following conclusion: what is precluded by assent is the recognition that there are reasonable grounds for the withholding of assent from *p*. What is precluded is the admission that it is 'reasonable' to doubt in this particular case. Newman's understanding of the independence and indubitability of assent can be summarized in his claim that

it is possible then, without disloyality to our convictions to examine their grounds, even though in the event they are to fail under the examination, for we have no suspicion of this failure. (194)

In this single passage Newman points to both the indubitability and the dubitability of assents: there is a 'consciousness' of the possibility of reversal but there is no 'suspicion' of failure; there is recognition that there is genuine dubitability (either merely logical or more-than-logical, depending on the interpretation adopted) but there is not 'reasonable' dubitability.

In this chapter I have studiously confined myself to Newman's discussion of doubt as it relates to assent, avoiding all references to doubt as it particularly relates to certitude. The following consideration of certitude proper will elaborate these conclusions, establishing the precise senses in which certitude is dubitable or indubitable.

CHAPTER

V

That kind of *Assent* which doth arise from such plain
and clear Evidence as doth not admit any reasonable
cause of doubting, is called *Knowledge* or *Certainty*.
John Wilkins, *Of the Principles and
Duties of Natural Religion*, 1675

In the preceding chapter I examined the kind of doubt
Newman considered incompatible with assent — namely, the
admission that it is reasonable to suspend or withhold assent
in a particular case — as well as the kind of dubitability of
assent implied by his recognition that assents could be rightly
overturned. Assents were seen to be criticizable even though
they were 'independent' of inference, and even though doubt
was incompatible. Certitude, however, may be a different
matter. Certitude is a *reflex* assent, a recognition of the
validity of our initial assent after a reasoning process. The
important question is how the reflex nature of certitude may
modify the admissions possible concerning dubitability and
corrigibility, and hence modify the possibility of criticism.

There are three prima-facie indications that the reflex
nature of certitude does preclude, for Newman, the criticizability that was possible in the case of simple assents. First,
Newman claims that certitudes are 'indefectible' or irreversible. Second, he claims that if we are certain we 'reject from
our minds, as out of the question, the very notion of our
being mistaken'. Third, he argues that, if called upon to do
so, we can legitimately make a 'formal promise' never to
change our belief.

These three claims provide support for a picture of uncriticizable religious commitment. I suggest, however, that an
examination of these claims reveals three aspects of Newman's
thought which can lead to an alternative picture of religious
commitment. I shall be arguing in this chapter and the next

that three independent aspects of Newman's thought reinforce one another and converge toward the conclusion that
there is an important strand in Newman's work — as yet inadequately recognized and appreciated — according to which
Newman's prohibition on doubt is not meant to and does not
entail ultimate immunity from criticism. I repeat that this is
not the only position on religious adherence to be found in
his work — but I am convinced that elaboration of it is a
necessary part of Newman exegesis and in addition can prove
fruitful for contemporary philosophy of religion by suggesting ways to reconcile rational and 'unconditional' commitment.

In discussing the certitude necessary to religious faith,
Newman declared that 'real "doubt" ' consists in a 'deliberate
withholding of assent to the Church's teaching';[1] it is a
'refusal to pronounce [the doctrine] true'.[2] To some critics
the prohibition on doubt implied that a Catholic 'never,
never can doubt again; that whatever his misgivings may be,
he must stifle them, nay, must start from them as the
suggestions of the evil spirit; in short that he must give up
altogether the search after truth, and do a violence to his
mind, which is nothing short of immoral'.[3] In the following
sections on kinds of commitment, indefectibility and dubitability I will analyse the kind of resistance to change that
Newman sees as part of genuine commitment.

1. The Persistence of Certitude — Two Kinds of Resistance

A. *Non-deliberate, Passive Commitment*

Newman gives an example from which we can start our
inquiry concerning the persistence that is part of certitude.
Let us suppose, he says, we decide to reconsider our initial
assent to the proposition that Napoleon the First was
deficient in heroism. We 'at length [as a result of informal
reasoning] find that the point is too clear to admit of any
dispute; we see there is no room, no corner, for a doubt, we
have no fear at all that we can be mistaken in maintaining it'.[4]

---

[1] *V.M. I*, p. 84, n.4.   [2] *V.M. I*, p. 108, n.2.
[3] *Mix.*, 'Faith and Doubt', p. 215.   [4] *T.P.*, p. 127 (25 Sept. 1865).

Thus, examination of our initial assents can lead to reflex assents to them, or to certitudes. When it does, such assents are accompanied by an increased persistence manifesting itself in implicit claims concerning the possibility of doubt or mistake.

This persistence, or intellectual tenacity, is evinced in resistance to change in belief. This resistance, moreover, is in past spontaneous rather than deliberately willed:

> No one can be called certain of a proposition, whose mind does not spontaneously and promptly reject, on their first suggestion, as idle, as impertinent, as sophistical, any objections which are directed against its truth. No man is certain of a truth, who can endure the thought of the fact of its contradictory existing or occurring; and that not from any set purpose or effort to reject that thought, but, as I have said, by the spontaneous action of the intellect. (197–8)

Certitude is therefore characterized by a *de facto* passive resistance to change in belief: 'What is contradictory to the truth, [or better, what is perceived to be such] with its apparatus of argument, fades out of the mind as fast as it enters it' (198). Counter objections do not spontaneously arise, nor do those that are presented to us have any real impact. They fade out in virtue of the assurance we have gained through examination, and not because we choose to reject them.[5]

This understanding of spontaneous resistance to change in belief is consistent with the conclusions of one modern psychological study of commitment.[6] This study accounts for such passive resistance in terms of the organization of our cognitions. In the process of being convinced or becoming certain our cognitions are organized and ordered in a self-protecting way. A *de facto* resistance to change in belief derives from a non-deliberate process in which cognitions salient to our beliefs organize themselves in a consistent manner 'such that inconsistent information (coming from an attack) is not easily assimilated'.[7] Thus, even before we deliberately resist, we are resistant. The believer is less susceptible to counter-information simply because it is less easily assimilable, and this resistance is spontaneous, without

---

[5] Cf. letter to Froude (rough draft, 9 Apr. 1863) in Harper, p. 150.

[6] Charles A. Kiesler, *The Psychology of Commitment* (New York: Academic Press, 1971).   [7] Ibid., p. 109.

any effort of will.

This process accounts for and reveals itself in what has traditionally been considered the 'inability' of the believer to imagine what would constitute forceful counter-evidence. I suggest that this is part of what is meant in Newman's claim that doubt is incompatible with certitude — i.e. descriptively, doubt simply does not coexist with it. There is, as Newman says, a spontaneous rejection of the thought of 'the fact of its contradictory existing or occurring'; we see 'no room for doubt' and we have no fear of mistake. In effect we have a non-deliberate adherence to the belief, a non-deliberate commitment to it. Newman's claims concern spontaneous attitudes to counter-evidence. These attitudes do not result from either an explicit intention or decision to refuse to consider counter-information, and therefore do not, in themselves, support a charge that Newman urges us to immunize our beliefs or certitudes against criticism. Only *deliberate* rejections could provide prima-facie support for such a charge. It is important, therefore, in any attempt to discover whether Newman considers certitudes to be criticizable, not automatically to put all of Newman's remarks about the rejection of the possibility of error into the category of deliberate rejections.

B. Deliberate, Active Commitment

Newman does, however, consider an active or deliberate commitment to be legitimate. We noted in the previous chapter that one of the roles of the will, according to Newman, was that of an active decision to affirm or confirm the certitude we in fact sometimes experience in concrete cases. This confirmation is a positive approval, rather than a mere recognition or assertion, of our certitude; it is equivalent to a deliberate commitment to maintain the certitude.

In a letter to Froude concerning his son Hurrell's conversion, Newman took it for granted that 'of course he intends to persevere and ought to intend, else he ought not to take so solemn a step'.[8] This intention need not take the form of a positive resolution or formal intention never to abandon our

---

[8] Harper, p. 128 (2 Jan. 1860).

beliefs. Belief, according to Newman, does not imply the presence of a

positive resolution in the party believing never to abandon that belief. What belief, as such, does imply is, not an intention never to change, but the utter absence of all thought, or expectation, or fear of changing. A spontaneous resolution never to change is inconsistent with the idea of belief; for the very force and absoluteness of the act of assent precludes any such resolution. (193)

The idea of a formal resolution is precluded by the force of our belief. We do not 'commonly determine not to do what we cannot fancy ourselves ever doing' (193). This seems to refer to what we have called spontaneous adherence. On the other hand, Newman continues, 'we should readily indeed make such a formal promise [never to change] if we were called upon to do so' (193). Thus, the spontaneous adherence we experience can be formalized into a 'positive resolution' or 'promise'.

I suggest that following Newman's example we can consider 'intention', 'resolution', and 'promise' as roughly equivalent. For our purposes we can overlook possible differences between the three for the following reasons: first, the affirmation we are considering is an explicit and deliberate intention or resolution; secondly, the nuance of obligation that generally attaches to promise is not significantly different in Newman's account for promise or formal intention or resolution; thirdly, we can bring the positive resolution closer to a promise by considering the promise as one made to oneself.

Thus, religious commitment, for Newman, involves two kinds of adherence or commitment, each related to a different kind of resistance to change in belief. Spontaneous resistance to change is an inevitable concomitant of the assurance that characterizes the passive adherence of certitude itself. In addition, an active confirmation of the certitude we experience is deemed necessary by Newman for a number of reasons (as we shall see) and this confirmation leads to various kinds of resistance to change in belief. The crucial question — given Newman's claims about the lack of room for doubt, the lack of fear of mistake and the legitimacy of a formal promise never to change — is whether the persistence and resistance Newman sees as part of religious commitment entails immunity to criticism. Our understanding of his view of genuine religious adherence will, therefore, depend on a further examination of his claims concerning the indefectibility and indubitability of certitudes.

2. The 'Indefectibility' Claim

Newman makes one claim at length in the *Grammar* — the claim that certitude is indefectible — which offers significant textual warrant for the charge that he prohibits the criticism of certitudes. In what follows I shall consider the claim that certitude is indefectible, arguing that although there are clearly two conflicting strands in the *Grammar* on the question of indefectibility, there is reason to believe that the admission of *defectibility* is consistent with other claims Newman makes regarding the dubitability of certitudes and the defeasibility of religious commitment. None of these three in itself provides conclusive evidence, but I suggest that they reinforce each other and converge toward the conclusion that there is an important strand in Newman's work — as yet inadequately appreciated — according to which certitudes and religious commitment are not uncriticizable.

The chapter on 'Complex Assent' illustrates the problem of indefectibility. On the one hand, certitude is termed an objectively true conviction (191) or a knowledge of the truth of our conviction (197). Certitudes are said to be not genuine unless they correspond with the truth; they are not real unless they are correct. But on the other hand, Newman immediately goes on to recognize a distinction he ought to maintain — the distinction between 'truth' and the individual's 'mental state' of certainty:

What is once true is always true, and cannot fail, whereas what is once known need not always be known, and is capable of failing . . . . If I am certain of a thing, I believe it will remain what I now hold it to be, even though my mind should have the bad fortune to let it drop. (197)

Similarly, he admits that a main characteristic of certitude is being confident that 'certitude will last, but . . . confident of this also, that, if it did fail, nevertheless, the thing itself, whatever it is, of which we are certain, will remain just as it is, true and irreversible' (199–200). Thus, real certitudes, it is admitted, can be lost, though the truth is immutable. In this chapter, therefore, we have a strand arguing the indefectibility of certitudes as well as a strand arguing the defectibility of them.

The chapter on the 'Indefectibility of Certitude' which follows in the *Grammar* does not consistently develop the indefectibility strand as one would expect from the title, but cultivates the contradiction by providing more material on both sides of the question. First, on the side of indefectibility, we are told that to be certain is to be possessed of a truth (221); certitudes that fail are only 'apparent' certitudes (222, 223). Though certitudes have no 'distinct', 'immediate', or 'interior' test (222, 255),[9] they have a negative test, that of indefectibility — 'whoever loses his certitude on a given point is thereby proved not to have been certain' (256).

Newman also gives a number of examples which are contrived to illustrate the claim to indefectibility. In one example, Newman urges us to consider three Protestants, one of whom becames a Catholic, one a Unitarian, and one an infidel. It is not true, he says, that they lost their old certitudes; rather each of them started with particular certitudes which they carried through into a new belief system, finding in the new one another expression of their previous certitudes (244 ff.). What look like changes in certitudes are really only additions to early certitudes. Since religion is in fact a complex of assents — some certitudes, some not (243) — and since two men could be Protestants while emphasizing different certitudes (since Protestantism means a hundred things (244)), it is possible for conversions to occur without a loss of certitudes; changes in accidental beliefs do not witness to the defectibility of certitude. Newman colourfully pushes this to an extreme, arguing that it is conceivable

that a man might travel in his religious profession all the way from heathenism to Catholicity, through Mahometanism, Judaism, Unitarianism, Protestantism, and Anglicanism without any one certitude lost, but with a continual accumulation of truths. (251)

What then are we to make of this kind of example? Newman apparently thinks that it proves that conversions never involve a loss of a genuine certitude; and he thinks he has

---

[9] *T.P.*, p. 121 (1865).

reached this conclusion without 'quibbling' (252), but it is clear that he has not supported the indefectibility claim. He has not shown that a conversion does not involve a loss of at least one certitude, nor that a genuine certitude is never lost.

In the very same chapter, however, where Newman has made explicit claims and given numerous examples to show that certitude is indefectible, he also makes several crucial admissions which lead to a claim that certitudes are *defect-ible*. He admits that 'any conviction, false as well as true, may last; and any conviction, true as well as false may be lost' (222). The claim to defectibility is also supported by remarks to the effect that the bell of our intellect can sound certainty when it should not (233). Certitude moreover, does not fail 'as a general rule' (221, 255); it does not fail 'on the whole' (240) or frequently (221). Scattered comments in letters also reveal an awareness of 'false' and 'antagonist' certitudes,[10] as well as a claim that 'of course there may be abuses and mistakes in particular cases of certitude'.[11]

That Newman makes conflicting claims in regard to the indefectibility of certitude cannot be denied. His zeal carried him at times into two false equations: (1) the equation of justified certitude with correct certitude, and (2) the equation of the state of an individual's mind with the norma-tive object, truth.[12] In the very same chapters that he makes these claims, however, he denies them as well. Both in these chapters and in scattered correspondence Newman recognizes that certitudes fail and that men make mistakes in their certitudes; he recognizes the distinction between the truth which cannot fail and certitudes which can fail, and he con-tinually qualifies the claim to indefectibility ('on the whole', 'as a general rule', etc.).

Several conclusions can be drawn. One can simply note the contradiction and leave it at that, claiming that it is impossible to decide between them. One can argue that, in spite of the

---

[10] Letter to Meynell, 17 Nov. 1869, cited by Zeno (p. 263); note that Meynell took Newman to be departing from philosophical tradition according to which certitude entails truth, and arguing, therefore, a defectible certitude (letter of 4 Nov. 1869); cf. also *G.A.*, p. 223.

[11] Ward II, p. 248 (letter to Wilberforce, 1868).

[12] Cf. J. A. Brunton, 'The Indefectibility of Certitude', *Downside Review* 86 (July 1968).

vacillation, Newman is for other reasons committed to the indefectibility claim. One can argue that Newman's continual qualifications of indefectibility effectively dissolve the claim altogether.[13] Finally one could suggest, as I do, that the defectibility strand is not an aberrant bit of material best ignored, but rather is a discussion which fits in well with at least two other aspects of Newman's thought on certitude which imply the criticizability of certitudes, and so contributes to an alternative picture of religious commitment. We will consider one of these other aspects in the following section.

3. The Dubitability of Certitudes

The second aspect of Newman's thought on certitude I want to consider is his set of claims concerning what I call the 'indubitability' and 'dubitability' of certitudes. Two of Newman's papers in preparation for the *Grammar* are especially instructive for this purpose — those of 20 July and 25 September 1865. In the first of these Newman describes the *indubitability* of certitudes as follows: certitude means that 'we do not at all admit the contrary idea; nay, that we cannot admit it without an effort of mind; that the very supposition of it is an absurdity. . . . We repel and reject the insinuation that there is the faintest chance of our being mistaken'.[14] In the same place he says certitude precludes the 'admission into the mind of the very supposition in any shape that it is misplaced as to its object'.[15] In the second paper we find the same refrain: if we are certain 'we reject from our minds, as out of the question, the very notion of our being mistaken'.[16]

These claims seem to refer to spontaneous tendencies of the mind, a spontaneous resistance to change, a spontaneous inability to doubt rather than to the deliberate exclusion of doubt. The question is whether this kind of indubitability of certitudes precludes criticism and abandonment of them. In other words, we want to determine whether Newman is

---

[13] Cf. I. T. Ker, 'Recent Critics of Newman's *Grammar*'.
[14] *T.P.*, p. 122 (20 July 1865).
[15] Ibid., p. 123.   [16] Ibid., p. 127.

attempting to legitimate an uncritical dogmatism based on the putative absolute indubitability, and hence incorrigibility, peculiar to reflex acts of certitude. The question is whether certitudes remain, for Newman, effectively immune to criticism. This question can be approached indirectly by looking at which kind of *dubitability* of certitudes, if any, Newman allows. Such dubitability would at least establish a necessary condition for criticizability.

Newman emphasizes the earlier claims about indubitability by concluding that 'we have ceased to be certain the very moment that we entertain the supposition that perhaps after all we are wrong'.[17] He immediately insists, however, that this does not rule out a number of admissions on our part:

in saying this I do not mean that we lose our certitude if we allow that in the abstract it is possible that we are wrong, or that there is a mathematical chance of it. Nor do I mean that we are no longer certain of a thing, if we admit its contradictory into our minds as a mere conception. ... nor is it inconsistent again with certitude to listen to arguments which tend to the denial of its object.

Thus, Newman appears to allow that a number of different types of concessions concerning the possibility of error are compatible with certitude.

We can admit that 'in the abstract it is possible that we are wrong'. This is an admission of fallibility; Newman clearly recognizes, in the *Grammar* at least, that certitude does not equal or require infallibility (224). This is not a trivial recognition on Newman's part — a century later it is still necessary to remind philosophers that certitude does not require infallibility and that conclusiveness does not require incorrigibility.[18] In addition we can allow the 'contradictory of it into our minds as a mere conception'. This probably is an admission of the fact that not-p is not logically contradictory — it can be conceived. Both these admissions at least preclude an intellectual closure which might have followed if they had been denied.

But the admission of fallibility and of the logical dubitability of our certitudes is not all that is compatible with certitudes. Newman admits that there can be a 'mathematical

---

[17] Douglas Greenlea, 'Unrestricted Fallibilism'.
[18] *T.P.*, p. 122 (20 July 1865).

chance' of our being wrong, as well as that there can be arguments produced against our certitudes. This latter admission especially makes it clear that Newman is allowing a 'genuine dubitability' of certitudes — reasons can be adduced against them; there is more to be said for not-*p* than that it is merely conceivable. Yet even this recognition is seen by Newman to be compatible with certitude.

I suggest that what underlies Newman's various restrictions and concessions concerning certitude is the awareness (noted earlier with respect to assent) that not all doubt that is possible (even more-than-logically possible) is necessarily reasonable in a given case. In other words, I suggest that the Wittgensteinian distinction discussed earlier is relevant here too as a way of illuminating Newman's understanding of the admissions allowed and precluded by certitude.

Newman's suggestion that to require absolute indubitability in order to have 'certainty' would effectively banish words like 'certainty' and 'necessity' from the language[19] has a very Wittgensteinian ring about it, reminding one of Wittgenstein's admonition to 'forget this transcendent certainty'.[20] That what Newman requires for certainty is the absence of reasonable doubt, not the absence of *all* possibility of doubt, is also supported by some important points in the *Grammar*. The situation where we 'can be certain, and ought to be certain' is one in which a 'reasonable conclusion' results from the union of a number of independent probabilities (291). Newman offers an extensive discussion of several examples of such 'reasonable' conclusions — in physics, law, and literary criticism. The example from the law courts (pp. 324-8) is especially significant since a number of modern authors have also used models of jurisprudence to illuminate the certainty possible in concrete questions.[21] Newman argues that in order to be decisive evidence against a criminal, the evidence must carry 'such a reasonableness, or body of implicit reasons for it in addition, as may exclude any probability, *really such,* that he is not guilty' (324, emphasis mine). In addition, 'speculative certitude' (326) rather than merely 'practical

---

[19] *Dev.*, p. 170.
[20] *On Certainty* § 47; cf. also § § 554, 663.
[21] E.g., John Wisdom, 'Gods' and Stephen Toulmin, *The Uses of Argument.*

certitude' is necessary and possible in legal cases; speculative certitude arises from a convergence of probabilities which 'constitute a real, though only a reasonable, not an argument-ative, proof' (327). Speculative certitude of *p* is attained when the jurors can rule out 'reasonable doubt' about not-*p* (325). This legal example is meant by Newman to illustrate the way in which speculative certitude can result from a cumulative, convergent case; it illustrates at the same time the way in which for Newman, as for Wittgenstein, to be certain was to be able to exclude, not all doubt, but all 'reasonable' doubt.

For Newman, admissions of certain kinds of dubitability do not determine or qualify our claims to certitude *here and now,* in this particular case — this is what I take him to mean by the phrase 'infallibility *pro hac vice*' (227). The reason-ableness of withholding assent is not determined simply by the logical dubitability of our certitudes. Moreover, it is not determined by the recognition that we *could* have reasons for doubting — this possibility does not introduce reasonable grounds for doubting in the particular case at hand. The reasonability or unreasonability of withholding assent, of saying that 'perhaps after all we are wrong', is a judgement made on the basis of the particular circumstances obtaining in a given case. In other words, Newman's distinctions between what is allowed by certitude and what is precluded by it suggest that he saw a difference similar to that pointed to by Alan R. White in his discussion of the modality of 'possibility'. White argues that 'sceptical arguments based on the premise that it is possible for something to be otherwise than it appears to be provide no reason for the conclusion that it is possible that something is otherwise than it appears to be.'[22] More precisely the difference is expressed as follows:

... the possibility which is excluded by certainty is the possibility of 'may', not the possibility of 'can'; that is, it is the possibility that some-thing *is* (or was or will be) so, not the possibility that it (should) be so or the possibility *for it to be so.*[23]

White's distinction between two kinds of possibility does in

[22] Alan R. White, *Modal Thinking* (Ithaca: Cornell University Press, 1975), p. 15. [23] Ibid., pp. 78–9.

fact seem to concur with what I take to be an acceptable intuition — namely, that there is a significant difference between admitting that it is possible that we *could* be wrong about a particular kind of matter and admitting that it is possible that we *are* wrong in this particular case.

The use of this distinction would be consistent with Newman's usage since what Newman ruled out was the supposition that our certitude *'is* misplaced'. What is precluded is the admission that 'perhaps after all we *are* wrong'. This may be what Newman is referring to when he claims that certitude precludes enduring 'the thought of *the fact* of its contradictory existing or occurring'.[24] The use of this distinction also allows Newman to consistently claim both that we reject the insinuation that 'there is the faintest chance of our being mistaken' and that we can recognize that there is a 'mathematical chance' of error, and even more, that there can be reasoned arguments against our certitude.

What is ruled out for Newman is that we admit 'the contradictory of what we have hitherto held as a fact, and that, deliberately'.[25] Since Newman sees the latter as 'seriously' entertaining the possibility of error, he must not mean simply that the admission of not-p is precluded (since if we were deliberately to admit not-p we would be denying p rather than 'seriously' entertaining the possibility of not-p). 'Seriously' entertaining the possibility of not-p is more likely equivalent, in White's terms, to admitting that it is possible in this case that 'something *is* otherwise than it appears to be'. The entertaining which is not prejudicial to certainty is the admission that it is *possible* that what we believe *could* be otherwise than it appears to be. Newman also correlates this here with the inquiring attitude: 'Not till I listen to arguments in opposition [to] my present belief in the spirit and temper of an inquirer, should I have lost my certitude in it.'[26]

In his essay 'Faith and Doubt' (1849) Newman expounds an understanding of the admissions which are inappropriate to someone while he is certain — an understanding which fits in well with the above suggestion. He explains why it is reasonable for the Church to forbid 'her children to entertain

---

[24] *G.A.*, pp. 197–8, italics mine; cf. also *T.P.*, p. 3 (14 Apr. 1853).
[25] *T.P.*, p. 122 (20 July 1865).   [26] Ibid., p. 123.

any doubt of her teaching' by giving examples of what such doubt would involve.[27] A 'real, though latent, doubt' is betrayed, for example, by someone who, 'after professing his certainty . . . added, that, for what he knew, he might doubt one day about [what he claimed to be certain]'.[28] He describes the state of mind which is incompatible with certitude as follows:

A person who says, 'I believe just at this moment, but perhaps I am excited without knowing it, and I cannot answer for myself, that I shall believe tomorrow', does not believe. A man who says . . . 'I believe as far as I can tell, but there may be arguments in the background which will change my view', such a man has not faith at all.[29]

To doubt, therefore, is to 'anticipat[e] a time when perhaps I shall not believe'. One 'cannot both really believe it now, and yet look forward to a time when perhaps I shall not believe it; to make provision for future doubt, is to doubt at present'.[30] Newman is arguing here that the criticism of the prohibition on doubt is equivalent to recommending that our faith in God always be 'attended with a *caveat,* on the worshipper's part, that he did not promise to render it tomorrow, that he would not answer for himself that some argument might not come to light, which he had never heard before, which would make it a grave moral duty in him to suspend his judgement and his devotion'.[31] Can real certainty, Newman asks, be qualified by the reservation that we 'may be allowed to doubt . . . at some future time'?[32]

It must be admitted that Newman ties up the Church's right to prohibit doubt with its claim to infallibility,[33] and it must also be admitted that occasionally Newman suggests that we need not re-examine what we have examined 'once for all'.[34] I nevertheless claim that the bulk of Newman's thought on doubt in this essay is directed to describing the psychological state that is incompatible with certainty — the hesitation, the tentativeness, and the fear. And in this respect he is correct — these attitudes are incompatible with a claim to certainty. Newman's examples of the doubt that is ruled

[27] *Mix.*, p. 216.   [28] Ibid.   [29] Ibid., pp. 216–17.
[30] Ibid.   [31] Ibid., p. 221.   [32] Ibid.   [33] Ibid., p. 230.
[34] Ibid., p. 224; on the other hand, he reproaches himself at one point for exercising 'more faith than criticism' in a matter (*Apo.* p. 184).

out suggest that he is most concerned here with claiming that certain admissions about future doubt effectively admit the reasonableness of doubt in the case at hand — 'to make provision for future doubt, is to doubt at present'.

His claim that 'he who really believes in it now, cannot imagine the future discovery of reasons to shake his faith'[35] resembles contemporary philosophical claims concerning the claims and concessions possible to one who is certain. For example, George Dicker suggests that certainty implies the believer's claim that he is sure that what in future might appear to be negative evidence will in fact be 'neutralizable', capable of being reinterpretated.[36] He describes the attitude implicit in certainty in a way very similar to Newman's:

If S is (absolutely) certain that *p*, then S is completely confident that there will be some explanation of any new data that seems to tell against *p* such that this data does not really tell against *p*.[37]

The incompatibility of doubt in this sense is said not to equal dogmatism. Alan R. White concurs, suggesting that what is true of the believer is that he 'cannot *see* how the claim could be invalidated'.[38] In itself, this does not mean that the believer refuses to allow it ever to be invalidated — there is a distinction between a description of a present attitude and an infallible prediction.[39] I suggest that this is often Newman's point in suggesting that doubt is incompatible with faith.

In summary, I have been suggesting that the admissions which Newman allows as compatible with certitudes do not necessarily qualify our certitude in a particular case. It may be more-than-logically possible to doubt *p*, yet be unreasonable to doubt it in a given case. However, these admissions

[35] Ibid., p. 219.

[36] 'Certainty Without Dogmatism: A Reply to Unger's "An Argument for Skepticism",' *Philosophical Exchange* 1 (Summer 1974).

[37] Ibid., p. 166.

[38] 'On Claiming to Know', in *Knowledge and Belief,* ed. A. Phillips Griffiths, pp. 103–4.

[39] In the *Apologia* Newman makes a very similar distinction (p. 148); cf. William A. Christian, *Meaning and Truth in Religion* (Princeton: Princeton University Press, 1964), esp. pp. 110–12. This is one way of reading Norman Malcolm's suggestion in 'Knowledge and Belief', reprinted in *Knowledge and Belief,* ed. A. Phillips Griffiths; Peter Unger takes an opposite interpretation of Malcolm's essay ('An Argument for Skepticism', *Philosophical Exchange* 1 (Summer, 1974)).

do leave room for the possibility of criticism. They are a necessary condition for criticizability. This conclusion fits in with the claims Newman makes concerning the defectibility of certitude. What remains to be seen is whether Newman actually allows the utilization of that room for criticism conceded by the admitted dubitability of certitudes, or whether, in spite of those admissions, he renders certitude immune to criticism, precluding counter-evidence from ever having an effect on certitudes.

On revelation being directed to a person and devotional and how this affects the question. You may
examine with your *will* determinatedly fixed. As
when a friend is accused, you do not let yourself
doubt him *at all,* till he is found guilty.

JHN, 27 March 1860

In Newman-like fashion I have been arguing that several
independent aspects of Newman's thought converge toward
the conclusion that religious certitudes are not uncriticizable.
I will now treat the third aspect, namely, a general view
found in Newman's work concerning the defeasibility of
religious commitment. We noted earlier that Newman considered a deliberate confirmation of the certitude we experience to be a legitimate action on our part. This could sometimes even take the form of a *promise* never to change. In
what follows I will discuss the extents and limits of this
deliberate commitment — in particular, why Newman judges
such a confirmation of our certitude (through intention or
promise) legitimate, and what kind of resistance it involves. I
will be arguing that the mode of adherence Newman requires
does not necessarily involve an indefeasible promise to maintain either a particular belief or religious commitment in
general.

1. The Intention to Adhere — Legitimation

An intention to maintain the belief and even a promise to
maintain it (if occasion arises for such a promise) are justified,
according to Newman, by the 'consciousness of my own
moral changeableness, and a fear, on that account, that I
might not be intellectually true to the truth' (199). All the
'moral motives' arising from age, condition, occupation,

fortune, etc. as well as prejudice can cause us to stifle our certitudes (168). Men may be 'biassed by their imaginations, or frightened by a deeper insight into the claims of religion upon the soul' (213) and so shrink back, giving up their beliefs. We must be careful to correlate our intellectual openness with our moral weakness. Newman's vivid realization of the weakness of men and the difficulties they face in maintaining beliefs which are not demonstrated yet are personally demanding, leads him to legitimate a more active form of adherence to our certitudes than the simple spontaneous resistance that is a part of them – namely, a deliberate (perhaps formal) commitment to accepting them as true without doubt.

Our intellectual instability should make us cautious, as well, since

reasons for assenting suggest reasons for not assenting ... objections and difficulties tell upon the mind; it may lose its elasticity, and be unable to throw them off. And thus, even as regards things which it may be absurd to doubt, we may, in consequence of some past suggestion of the possibility of error, or of some chance association to their disadvantage, be teased from time to time and hampered by involuntary questionings, as if we were not certain, when we are. (217)

He explains in a letter to Froude that because of the lack of logical completeness in concrete proofs, 'it is always also possible, perhaps even plausibly to resist a conclusion, even tho' it be one which all sensible men consider beyond question'.[1] In a letter to Wilberforce he notes similar reasons for legitimating an active commitment – we can always 'tease' ourselves, neurotically reminding ourselves of our fallibility. We all know, he says, 'what command nervous persons are obliged to exert over themselves lest they should doubt whether even they see or feel; or whether they know anything at all'.[2] A host of questions 'must be deliberately put aside, as beyond reason' (218).[3] The 'shreds and tatters of former controversies, and the litter of an argumentative habit, may beset and obstruct the intellect'; they must be 'put down' by the 'exercise of good sense and ... strength of will' (218).

[1] Harper, p. 208 (29 Apr. 1879). [2] Ward II, p. 249 (1868).
[3] Cf. Harper, p. 130 (15 Jan. 1860), where Froude notes that it is legitimate to require that inquirers not 'go out of their depth in inquiry'.

Both moral and intellectual considerations may justify us, therefore, in affirming or stabilizing our certitudes. We can have a conviction (which we did not create) that it would be unreasonable, idiotic, not to be certain about *p,* but we could stifle it. As we noted in Chapter III, one of Newman's critics supported Newman in this respect, albeit unwittingly. In an idiom very similar to Newman's, Leslie Stephen wrote that 'It is our duty to believe what appears to us to be proved.'[4]

His example bears repeating:

> I may know that I am absolutely safe when I am at the brink of a precipice, but my body declines to be convinced, and shudders and turns giddy in spite of conclusive evidence. A demonstration may be as clear to me as a proposition of Euclid; but fear of authority, or dread of consequences, or mere blind sympathy with others, may prevent its real assimilation. To believe what we know to be certain at times even requires a kind of intellectual heroism.[5]

Newman suggests that precisely because this kind of situation is possible, we should complement the assurance we have with a commitment to hold the proposition without reserve. It is necessary and legitimate, because we are both weak and certain. A positive evaluation of adherence to our certitudes results in an intention or promise to adhere, to resist change or fickleness. An intention may be necessary if we are to maintain our beliefs long enough to do justice to all the evidence, both challenged and challenging. As we shall see, however, an intention to resist change is not necessarily an intention to resist change no matter what; it can require certain ways of resisting and not others.

2. Content of Resistance

Newman's early lectures on 'Christianity and Scientific Investigation' in the *Idea of a University* provide some background to his view of the deliberate resistance he sees as legitimate.[6] One form such resistance can take is that of a deliberate decision to *wait,* a refusal to be 'hasty' in giving in to objections. The philosophy of the 'imperial intellect' has in it several crucial maxims:

---

[4] *An Agnostic's Apology,* 'The Skepticism of Believers', p. 46.
[5] Ibid., p. 47.   [6] *Idea,* pp. 343-61 (1855).

(1)   'that truth cannot be contrary to truth'
(2)   'that truth often *seems* contrary to truth'
(3)   'the practical conclusion that we must be patient with such appearances and not be hasty to pronounce them to be really of a more formidable character'.[7]

The real believer is confident that if something seems to contradict revealed truth, it will turn out either that the former is not proven, or that it is not contradictory, or that it does not contradict something that is 'really revealed' in the first place.[8]

The resistance that is appropriate, therefore, involves a refusal to be hasty in pronouncing objections overwhelming:

If at the moment, it appears to be contradictory, then [the believer] is content to wait; knowing that error is like other delinquents; give it rope enough and it will be found to have a strong suicidal propensity.[9]

What Newman is here suggesting is that it is not necessarily more rational to be *totally open* to new and contradictory evidence, nor, *a fortiori*, to require a constant vigilance for counter-objections. In this he was opposed to people like Froude, for whom the only legitimate attitude to science or religion was the following:

though I think I see my way clearly, it is nevertheless possible that I may be wrong, I will therefore continue to be on the lookout for whatever may show whether I have been right or wrong.[10]

Froude suggested, further, that one must deliberately and imaginatively maintain the possibility of error before one. It is always necessary for a person

to keep before his eyes his knowledge of the fallibility of his processes of thought and those of advisors, and to maintain as vivid a recollection of the probabilities which lie against his conclusion, however small they may seem, as of the preponderating mass of probabilities in favour of it.[11]

Newman rejected Froude's requirements. His response was that such tentativeness — being always 'on the look out' and keeping before oneself a 'vivid' idea of the contrary probabilities — would have to be deliberately and artifically introduced by the believer, and that there was no reason to introduce it; the natural result of certitude is precisely that

---

[7] Ibid., p. 347.   [8] Ibid., p. 351.   [9] Ibid.
[10] Harper, p. 121 (letter to Newman, 29 Dec. 1859).
[11] Ibid., p. 120.

lack of qualification or hesitation.

Because Froude saw a 'residuum of doubt' in all non-demonstrable matters, he claimed that although we could be confident, we must always temper this with the recognition that

this is for the present the best conclusion I can come to, but ... I declare that I shall be at all times ready to reconsider it, if reasonably called on to do so. ... Nay, I shall be anxious to reconsider it, exactly in proportion as I have grave reason to expect that honest reconsideration will lead me to abandon it.[12]

The declaration Froude exacted — 'if reasonably called on to do so' — might have been literally acceptable to Newman, but the state of mind Froude thought it generated was not. The declaration that we 'shall be ready' and 'anxious to reconsider' was, for Froude, ideally an ever present conscious phenomenon. According to Newman, if a man 'professes to keep his mind open to change on a point if evidence comes ... he therefore implies that the thing in question may perhaps turn out in the event not true';[13] thus, I am 'anxious' to reconsider only in proportion as I have reason to suspect error — and I have at present absolutely no sufficient reason to suspect such error.

Given that Newman did recognize human fallibility and the corrigibility of beliefs, including 'genuine dubitability', it seems plausible to conclude that the major objection Newman had to Froude's formulations lay in their psychological overtones and implications. One can, according to Newman, admit fallibility and corrigibility without having to therefore be on the 'look-out', vividly remembering all the probabilities against one's belief, or considering one's conclusion as 'the best I can come to' *for the present*. If Froude required the admission of corrigibility of all beliefs, then Newman could grant him that easily enough. But that kind of corrigibility implied no psychological reservation; it has no concomitant of fear or hesitation or tentativeness. If Froude required the latter, he, according to Newman, was asking for what was appropriate only to an admission that doubt is reasonable in the particular case.

Froude objected to *discarding* the 'residuum of doubt' that

---

[12] Ibid., pp. 120–1.   [13] *T.P.*, p. 3 (14 Apr. 1853), italics mine.

necessarily attached to concrete beliefs.[14] Newman was arguing, on the contrary, that logical incompleteness or an admission of corrigibility did not generate a residuum of doubt. The question was not whether such doubt should be discarded — doubt which operated in our reasoning was effectively discarded in the very process of reasoning and reaching certitude in the first place. It was a question of whether doubt should be introduced, whether the admission of corrigibility should be allowed to be constructed into a source of doubt since the mind, after all, could stifle certitude. Here he diverged from Froude, since Newman could simply find no sufficient reason for this introduction of doubt.

Froude foreshadowed the charge later made by Bartley that we are irrationally committed to our beliefs unless we continually attack them. In rejecting the need to be on the 'look-out' and to attack our convictions continually, Newman recognized, though not explicitly, that certain rational considerations can justify intellectual resistance to change in belief. For Froude, the will had 'no function in reference to the formation and maintenance of our "Belief", but that of insisting that all probabilities on either side shall be honestly regarded and weighed and borne in mind'.[15] For Newman, the will does have a role to play in the maintenance of certitude, at least in terms of simple tenacity. Moreover, that role should not be understood as going against intellectual judgement.[16]

Newman argued, against Froude, that intellectual tenacity was reasonable. The fact that one's present system of beliefs coheres well and that one would have to make radical adjustments in it in order to accept a challenging belief, provides in itself a prima-facie reason for giving the challenged belief the benefit of the doubt. If a currently held belief 'dovetail[s]'[17] with the core of our belief system, we have a right to 'deliberately put aside' what seem to us to be 'no thoroughfares' (218). Froude was arguing for an anti-dogmatic under-

[14] Harper, p. 120 (letter to Newman, 29 Dec. 1859).
[15] Ibid., p. 121.   [16] Cf. Harper, p. 208 (29 Apr. 1879).
[17] *T.P.*, p. 19 (16 Dec. 1853).

standing of scientific inquiry, where scientific honesty required total openness to criticism. By urging a principle of tenacity, Newman, on the other hand, was presaging a later development in the philosophy of science which would over-turn this 'naive falsificationism'.

This development is made explicit in the work of Imre Lakatos, for example, a contemporary philosopher of science who argues for 'tenacity' and the 'rationality of a certain amount of dogmatism' in science.[18] Science is construed by him in terms of 'research programmes' which have a conven-tionally designated 'hard core' surrounded by a protective belt of auxiliary hypotheses. This protective belt gets con-tinually readjusted and perhaps even replaced in an effort to maintain the 'hard core'. This goes on while theoretical and empirical progress is being generated; it can even go on in the face of a degenerating problem shift — *for a while*. The determination of how much tenacity is appropriate and rational, i.e. how much degeneration is too much, is not a simple matter. It depends not only on observational anomalies, but also on the possibility of a relevantly suitable alternative theory. The impact of counter-evidence is qualified by the fact that we are concerned, not with isolatable theories, but with complexes of interrelated hypo-theses of different status. The point is that the degree of openness that is rational is not determinable *a priori*.

The analogy with religion is significant (though not exact).[19] Newman noted that 'religion is not a proposition, but a system; it is a rite, a creed, a philosophy, a rule of duty, all at once . . . it is a collection of . . . various kinds of assents, at once and together, some of one description, some of another' (243). Since neither the challenge nor what is challenged is a simple unit, the principle of conservatism is as necessary and fruitful in religion as in science.

[18] Imre Lakatos, 'Falsification and the Methodology of Scientific Research Programmes', in *Criticism and the Growth of Knowledge*, eds. Imre Lakatos and Alan Musgrave (Cambridge: University Press, 1970), pp. 91–189 (quoted words are from pp. 174–5).

[19] Cf. William Austin, 'Religious Commitment and the Logical Status of Doctrines', and Ian Barbour, *Myths, Models and Paradigms* (New York: Harper & Row, 1974) for considerations of the differences, as well as similarities, in the analogy between religious and scientific commitment.

This principle of conservatism leads to the tenacity which is the heart of Newman's 'magisterial intolerance of any contrary assertion' (199). This can take an even more active form, namely an attempt to undermine contrary arguments or show them to be inadequate. In a passage we noted earlier, Newman continued to describe intellectual tenacity by saying that we are justified not only in waiting, but even in 'encouraging, in helping forward the prospective suicide'.[20] We can 'not only give the error rope enough', we can 'show it how to handle and adjust the rope'. Rational openness need not require that we treat all opposing evidence as innocent until proven guilty. Beliefs which we are certain of may deserve the benefit of the doubt not only in the sense that it is right to be tenacious, but also in the sense that it is legitimate to attempt to find weaknesses in counter-evidence. Newman requires that we treat opposing arguments fairly — 'when objections come before you, consider them fairly; but don't begin with doubting'.[21] But an honest attempt to assess the merits of counter-material is not only compatible with but seems to require a sincere search for its most serious demerits as well.

Froude thought Newman was attempting to legitimate the following intellectual attitude: 'I always *will* hold this — I *will* earnestly *endeavour* to combat any arguments brought forward against it and will resist the inclination to be swayed by them'.[22] He objected vigorously, arguing that such an attitude was not even legitimate in science. Newman had, after all, legitimated a formal promise never to change. Was Newman's commitment an 'I always will hold this'-commitment? Could such a commitment be compatible with rational requirements? Was it an indefeasible obligation to maintain the belief at all costs?

An intention or promise to adhere is not necessarily an intention to resist change in any and all cases; there can be

[20] *Idea*, p. 351.
[21] Harper, p. 208 (29 Apr. 1879); cf. *G.A.*, p. 199, where Newman claims that when we are certain we have no call on us to listen to the arguments of others, and can say to them 'Retro Satana' lest they tempt us from the truth. But remarks like these have to be read in light of a larger picture which urges us to treat objections 'fairly'.
[22] Harper, p. 135 (letter to Newman, 25 Jan. 1860).

limits to the resistance involved. That Newman recognized that there must be limits is suggested by Newman's view of his own change to Catholicism. Looking back at his conversion, he remarked that

So far from my change of opinion having any fair tendency to unsettle persons as to truth and falsehood viewed as objective realities, it should be considered whether such change is not *necessary*, if truth be a real objective thing, and be made to confront a person who has been brought up in a system *short* of truth. Surely the *continuance* of a person who wishes to go right, in a wrong system, not his *giving it up*, would be that which militated against the objectiveness of Truth.[23]

This claim, coupled with Newman's admission that there is no infallible test for determining genuinely true certitudes, implies that Newman cannot consistently require that we insulate our certitudes totally. That he does not require this is corroborated by our conclusion that his admissions concerning the dubitability compatible with certitude allow for the possibility of criticism.

One of the limits of resistance noted by Newman concerns the occasion of resistance. When Newman claims that we have a right to 'deliberately put aside, as beyond reason' certain questions or difficulties, he insists that this is only allowed 'after the best use of reason' (218). Another limit concerns the way in which people should consider objections. We saw that he urged us to treat opposing arguments fairly — 'When objections come before you, consider them fairly but don't begin with doubting.' Asking himself how people should bear themselves toward objections to revelation, for example, Newman replies: 'Should they allow themselves fairly to examine? I say, yes, if it *comes* in their way and they have a duty to do so.'[24] Thus, although 'they will feel as a person having to examine the Newtonian hypothesis', i.e. 'confident', they can examine objections fairly.

There is in fact, he notes, a 'broad principle' which suggests that we can afford to listen to objections if we are certain: 'to fear argument is to doubt the conclusion, and to be certain of a truth is to be careless of objections to it' (203). We must not be intellectually 'tolerant' of objections (199),

---

[23] *Apo.*, p. 186.
[24] *T.P.*, p. 91 (27 Mar. 1860); *T.P.*, p. 122–3 (20 July 1865).

because of the moral and intellectual weakness noted earlier, but we still need to treat objections fairly. Too much closure indicates a lack of assurance; 'irritation and impatience of contradiction, vehemence of assertion, determination to silence others, — these are tokens of a mind which has not yet attained the tranquil enjoyment of certitude' (201). Our right to 'magisterial intolerance' is, therefore, qualified.

Newman suggests that it is not inconsistent with certitude to listen to opposing arguments since even 'unbelievers may be quite fair to this or that proof in behalf of the (occurrence or the) fact of miraculous occurrences, and yet remain all along steady ⟨in⟩ to their unbelief'.[25] We should consider further precisely what Newman means here by 'steady' since it will reveal a third limit to resistance which has significant implications for Newman's idea of genuine religious adherence.

3. Mode of Adherence

The mechanisms of intellectual resistance that have been treated above are means of insuring that we adhere long enough to do justice to the seriousness of the issues involved and to the convictions generated by the reflection which preceded our reflex assent of certitude. But can we be appropriately 'steady' in our certitudes without undertaking an indefeasible obligation to maintain the belief at all costs? Here the question of indefectibility is approached from another angle.

The kind of adherence that is necessary in religion is in part determined by the character of religious belief, which is in part determined by its object. Long before writing the *Grammar* Newman had attempted to find the fault in Froude's criticisms, concluding finally that there was a 'deeper philosophy' on the subject than Froude's, if only he could develop it. At the time he knew only that 'much lies in the meaning of the words certainty and doubt, much again in our duties to a *person,* as e.g., a friend'.[26] Eight years later in the process of writing the *Grammar* Newman filled this in

[25] *T.P.,* p. 123 (20 July 1865).　　　[26] Harper, p. 127 (2 Jan. 1860).

somewhat. In a letter to Wilberforce, he considered the question 'whether you may or may not rationally keep your mind *open* to change on a point on which your *phronesis* has already told you to decide one way'.[27] His conclusion was that there was a difference, with significant implications, between beliefs in science and beliefs in religion:

Does not nature, duty and affection teach us that a difference is to be made between things and persons? Ought I to be as open to listen to objections brought to me against the honour, fidelity, love towards me of a friend, as against the received belief that the earth is 95 million miles from the Sun?

Does the fact that there is a difference between commitment to persons and things mean that, for Newman, personal commitment should never be abandoned, that personal commitment can rightly be held at all costs?

It has been suggested in a contemporary discussion on religious belief and commitment that because religious commitment is personal, it must be 'boundless'. Edward F. Mooney, in 'Assertion and Commitment in Religious Belief', suggests that the 'lover vows to stay with his beloved *"through anything"*, "come what may", "come Hell or high water".'[28] A genuine personal commitment, therefore, would preclude the admission that there could be bounds to one's fidelity.

Can a personal commitment, if genuine, be other than a 'come what may', indefeasible commitment? Newman's answer is found in his comprehensive and final letter to Froude, which elaborates the mode of resistance he saw as appropriate and necessary for believers:

Arguments may overcome the Christian and he may give up his faith, but *till such a strong conclusion has overtaken him*, he will by an act of the will reject, it will be his duty, as well as his impulse to reject, all doubts, as a man rejects doubts about his friend's truth.[29]

In this same letter he argues that a man 'may *at length* be obliged to pronounce against his friend', but until he does he must not seriously entertain doubts about him.[30] Although we must consider objections fairly, it may nevertheless be

---

[27] Ward II, p. 250 (1868).   [28] *Sophia* 10 (Apr. 1971), p. 10.
[29] Harper, p. 209 (29 Apr. 1879), italics mine.
[30] Ibid., italics mine.

required of us that we put aside '*at least for the time,* real difficulties'.[31]

I suggest that Newman is arguing for a particular model of adherence in the case of certitude — a model of resistance which is compatible with rational abandonment of certitude. That is, Newman, in these kinds of passages at least, is attempting to preclude a particular kind of abandonment of certitude, just as he attempted to preclude a particular kind of abandonment of assent — namely, abandonment by degrees. The same independence which, as we saw earlier, was thought by Newman to be essential and sufficient for assent, could be sufficient even for certitude. That is, there can be no *direct* dependence on the reasons such as would lead to gradual change. That this is Newman's foremost concern is evidenced in his claim that a characteristic of certitude is that it

cannot be *immediately* dependent on the reasons which are its antecedents ... because if it were the direct result of sight, or testimony, or argument, then as it has been gradually created by them, *so might it be gradually destroyed, and each objection would weaken it according to its own force.*[32]

Newman also notes that whether the difficulties are great or small, 'if they went so far as to affect it at all, they would destroy it altogether'.[33]

Having considered in the preceding chapter the claims Newman made concerning the defectibility and dubitability of certitudes, it does not seem implausible to conclude that what is implied in the unconditionality of certitude is formally similar to what is implied in the unconditionality of assent — namely, an adherence that can be justifiably abandoned but only as a whole. Newman's conclusion that 'As soon as I entertain the objections adduced in a particular case as really telling, not upon the proof, but on the fact itself which is the object of my certitude, then, I am no longer certain at all'[34] does not preclude the rational abandonment of certitude. Newman's references to the defeasible commitment we owe to friends strongly support the conclusion,

[31] Ibid., p. 208, italics mine.
[32] *T.P.*, pp. 123–4 (20 July 1865), italics mine.
[33] Ibid., p. 123. [34] Ibid.

therefore, that even in personal commitments we may 'at length' be obliged to abandon our certitude; arguments may eventually cause us to give it up. His point, however, is that in the meantime an adherence that is strong and entire is necessary and legitimate.

Moreover, it should be noted that Newman supports the extrapolation from human friend to Divine Friend. The parallel is implicit throughout his comments on the subject, but at times it is unmistakable. For example, in discussing a proposed book in 1860 Newman described as follows a chapter on Revelation as being 'devotional': 'You may examine with your will determinatedly fixed. As when a friend is accused, you do not let yourself doubt him *at all,* till he is found guilty.'[35] We should note the phrase 'at all' — a reference to manner of adherence — but we should equally well note the phrase 'till he is found guilty'. Newman implies that we can finally be forced to admit his guilt — we are not being urged by him to commit ourselves blindly, even when our commitment is to a friend. Since Newman is talking about Revelation here, it seems that this norm is applicable even when the friend is divine. In either case irrational dogmatism does not seem to be the ideal put before us, even though it is stressed that the personal nature of the relationship requires a special adherence.

The kind of thing I think Newman had in mind is explored by a contemporary philosopher of religion who argues that a 'personal' commitment need not and should not be 'unbounded', although we do not need to be able to specify falsifying conditions.[36] That is, we cannot imagine what would cause us to give up our belief, but it is nevertheless possible that in a given situation we could *recognize* something as sufficient warrant for changing our commitment. We can regard a personal commitment 'as renounceable, and renounceable on particular grounds — grounds, though, which might not have been discoverable but for the particular falling-out situation's having actually arisen'.[37] Commitments can be considered 'renounceable' even though 'in virtue of

---

[35] *T.P.*, p. 91 (27 Mar. 1860); also see *G.A.*, p. 421.
[36] Joel Rudinow, 'Religious Commitment I', *Sophia* 12 (Apr. 1973).
[37] Ibid., p. 4.

their being personal, the reasons for their renunciation are not formulable, and hence not formulated, as hypothetical renunciation conditions, while the commitments are still held and in force'.[38] Another philosopher of religion, Basil Mitchell, offers an account of the tension between tenacity and criticism in religious commitment which, on at least one reading, can be understood according to the model which I have suggested underlies these quotations from Newman.[39]

It is appropriate here to refer to a criticism of Newman made by his contemporaries. Fitzjames Stephen, for example, argued that Newman's defence of indirect assent to propositions through assenting to the authority of the one who gives testimony was inadequate; he concluded that Newman confused assent to authority with assent to propositions.[40] The limits of such a criticism should be noted, however. First, assent to a proposition of which we apprehend only the predicate 'is true' is not the whole of religious faith for Newman, but rather is *one* kind of assent involved. Secondly, Newman disavows concern in the *Grammar* with the question of grounds for accepting the authority in question (16, 100). Since Newman allows a natural theology[41] and since he clearly states that we must 'know' about God before we can love or trust Him (120), his failure to distinguish adequately between assent to an apprehended proposition and assent to an authority's claim that a proposition which we do not apprehend is true is not in itself a failure to recognize the distinction between and logical priority of propositional 'belief-that' over 'belief-in' a person. In other words, the criticism of Newman as having a 'fideistic' commitment because it is personal does not seem warranted.

I have argued that the intention or promise that Newman legitimates is, therefore, not equivalent to undertaking an indefeasible obligation to maintain *p* 'come what may'.[42] This

---

[38] Ibid.   [39] *The Justification of Religious Belief.*

[40] 'On a Theory of Dr. Newman's as to Believing in Mysteries', Metaphysical Society paper of 12 Jan. 1875, cited by James Livingston in *The Ethics of Belief: An Essay on the Victorian Religious Conscience,* pp. 23–4.

[41] *Apo.,* p. 31, and *G.A.,* pp. 98, 100, 389–408.

[42] Also see Chap. VII for elaboration.

can be understood in terms of a distinction between formal and material promise. The claim by a believer that he 'knows' is a claim made from his side of the picture. As a result of the informal reasoning he has·gone through, the believer judges himself to have sufficient evidence for making a knowledge claim — a claim that his belief is true and appropriately justified. This claim is not compatible with certain other admissions — e.g. the believer cannot say 'I know but I am hesitant' or 'I know but I am unsure'.[43] But he can both say that he knows and that there is no infallible test for discriminating knowledge from putative knowledge. His claim to knowledge, therefore, admittedly entails nothing about the truth of the belief.

This last point is adequately recognized by Newman in his admissions that there is no immediate test for determining and distinguishing true and false certitudes.[44] This should (and usually does) influence his view of the limits of a legitimate intention or promise not to change. Being 'true to the truth' (193, 199) would seem to be the only thing that can warrant an indefeasible obligation which is nevertheless rational. It is, moreover, sufficient for religious commitment.

The formal promise or intention is therefore that of being true to the truth; it is non-specific. The material promise or intention to maintain p is the concrete instance of our formal promise at a given time, contingent on our continuing to judge that p expresses the truth. Should we, in spite of our intention to maintain p, come to believe, as a result of informal reasoning and convergent probabilities, that not-p is true, our formal promise to be true to the truth would receive a different content. The formal promise, therefore, is an indefeasibly obligating expression, while the material promise is subject to the all-or-nothing manner of adherence

---

[43] There is a full spectrum of opinions on the question of the necessity of the condition of 'confidence' with respect to 'knowing'. Norman Malcolm claims that 'being confident is a necessary condition of knowing' ('Knowledge and Belief', in *Knowledge and Belief*, p. 70). Andrew Zvara suggests that being sure is not necessary for a claim to know ('On Claiming to Know and Feeling Sure', pp. 272–4); A. D. Woozley, however, argues that although feeling sure is not a necessary condition for knowledge, it is a necessary one for a *claim* to know ('Knowing and Not Knowing', in *Knowledge and Belief*).

[44] *G.A.*, pp. 221, 255; *T.P.*, p. 121 (1865).

discussed earlier.

In conclusion, religious commitment, for Newman, involves persistence in two ways. Part of the persistence Newman sees as legitimate and necessary for religious believers is a spontaneous resistance to change in belief — a resistance which is an inevitable concomitant of the process of reaching certitude. In addition to this non-intentional adherence Newman argues that a confirmation of the certitude we experience may be necessary because we can stifle it. Newman thereby tries to legitimate a deliberate commitment, which can find expression in a variety of forms of resistance to change. The conditions and limits of this active deliberate commitment have been examined in this chapter, and warrant has been provided for the claim that although the personal relationship in religious commitment modifies the mode of adherence, it does not necessitate an indefeasible promise, obligation or intention to maintain the commitment 'come what may'. Together with part of Newman's thought on the defectibility of certitudes, and his position on the dubitability of certitudes, this understanding of the mode and limits of religious adherence yields a picture of religious commitment which can be seen as an alternative to that picture which follows from the claim that certitudes are indefectible and indubitable. This alternative picture, moreover, contributes to contemporary approaches to the problem of religious commitment as much as it contributes to studies of Newman's thought in itself.

CHAPTER

VII

The Romanist may investigate, but his conclusions are
ready-made. And so the Church of Rome stifles
thought; puts a premium on ignorance; is in open conflict with science; perpetuates its dogmas by making it
sinful to call them in question.

Review of the *Grammar of Assent, The Biblical
Repertory and Princeton Review*, April 1871

In the preceding chapters I have examined Newman's view of
religious belief and certitude as presented especially in the
Grammar. I have argued that according to Newman such
religious belief can be characterized by a total certainty. His
understanding of the character of our concrete attainment of
certitudes precludes the necessity of bridging a gap between
inference and certitude in any way distinct from the actual
process of reasoning itself; it is an entire, though human,
certainty. My conclusion concerning the relation of the will
to certitude was that at times Newman's reference to an 'act
of will' was a way of highlighting the quality of personal
appropriation involved in reaching certitude in concrete
cases; at other times it was a way of highlighting the deliberate affirmation of the certitude we in fact experience in such
cases. At no time was it a reference to a decision to become
certain, or to a decision which effects or completes certainty.
His distinction between judging that we ought to be certain
and being certain was therefore a distinction between
experiencing certitude and affirming it, rather than a distinction between seeing we ought to be certain and deciding to
become certain.

It is, strictly speaking, religious belief rather than faith that
has been under discussion thus far, since Newman limited his
concern in the *Grammar* to what it is to believe in religious
doctrines, excluding any discussion of faith since that would

involve believing in doctrines 'expressly because God has revealed them' (99–100). In an 1853 paper on faith and certainty Newman calls this religious belief *'fides acquisita'* and *'fides humana'*, and contrasts it with *'fides divina'*.[1] The former is possible purely naturally; the latter depends on God's gift of grace.[2] In this chapter I want to qualify and extend my understanding of Newman's view of the affirmation of certitude necessary in genuine religious belief, considering the relation of divine faith to this affirmation, both in terms of the object of the affirmation and the kind of adherence involved.

1. Certitude, Commitment, and the Gift of Grace

Ambiguity concerning the relation of divine faith and the affirmation of certitude we have been considering in previous chapters is apparent in a letter Newman wrote to Mrs Froude, in which he attempted to explicate a 'right notion of how to gain faith':

It is, we know, the Gift of God, but I am speaking of it as a human process and attained by human means. Faith then is not a conclusion from premises, but the result of an act of the *will*, following upon a *conviction* that to believe is a duty. . . . For directly you have a conviction you ought to believe, reason has done its part and what is wanted for faith is, not proof, but *will*.[3]

In speaking of an act of the will following on a conviction that to believe is a duty, Newman is referring to an act of the will affirming our human certitude. The restriction of his concern to faith 'as a human process and attained by human means' might suggest that he equates faith with *fides acquisita*. He would in that case be clearly discussing the affirmation we considered earlier. On the other hand, he could be referring to the human side of faith, divine faith considered as human process. What is really a gift of grace requires for its human expression, or manifests itself to us as, a decision to affirm the certainty we have experienced. On this latter view, however, there is a further ambiguity. *Fides divina* might be simply the affirmation of human certitude,

[1] *T.P.*, p. 38 (16 Dec. 1853).   [2] Ibid., p. 37.
[3] Harper, p. 77 (27 June 1848).

through grace, and therefore co-extensive with the affirmation we spoke of earlier. That particular affirmation would assume a distinctive quality when done through grace. *Fides divina*, however, might instead refer to a different affirmation, over and above that.

A second passage reinforces the ambiguity. In the essay 'Faith and Private Judgment', Newman notes: 'the two things are quite distinct from each other, seeing you ought to believe and believing'.[4] This might appear to counter my earlier conclusion that the judgement that we ought to be certain of *p* is not separable from the unconditional acceptance of *p*; that is, seeing we ought to be certain of *p* is equivalent to experiencing certainty of *p*. However, Newman continues, the two things are quite distinct because 'reason, if left to itself will bring you to the conclusion that you have sufficient grounds for believing, but belief is the gift of grace'. He thus equates 'believing' with divine faith. In another paper on certainty Newman had claimed that 'belief' was the peculiar characteristic of divine faith; at the same time, however, he admitted that we can have certainty prior to this kind of 'belief':

[Our] assent to, or speculative evident judgment of, the credibilitas of Revelation is followed by the act of reflexion upon, or recognition of, that assent, which I have called *certainty*. .... A mind [however] which gets as far as this *does not yet believe*.[5]

Seeing that we ought to believe could therefore be quite distinct from divine 'belief' or faith while being identical with our ordinary sense of 'belief', including believing with certainty. Thus, this claim is compatible with my previous conclusion. It raises, however, the problem of the distinctive character of divine faith, since Newman had prefaced this particular claim as follows:

There are, to be sure, many cogent arguments to lead one to join the Catholic Church, but they do not force the will. We may know them, and not be moved to act upon them. We may be quite convinced without being persuaded.[6]

---

[4] *Mix. I*, p. 212.

[5] *T.P.*, p. 37, italics mine. Note that his conclusion that the judgement is credible does not mean that it is merely capable of being believed, but that it ought to be believed (cf. paper on 'Nature and Cause of Faith', 1848, cited by Pailin, *The Way to Faith*, p. 208).   [6] *Mix. I*, p. 212.

The distinction between 'being convinced' and 'being persuaded' may strike us at first as a pseudo-distinction. Elsewhere, however, Newman defines 'persuasion' as

an opinion or the belief about an alleged fact or truth ... with a determination ⟨maintenance/belief⟩ that it can not be otherwise ⟨never to think otherwise/that that belief will continue⟩.[7]

Persuasion appears to be something like a determination to maintain the belief; it can then be naturally contrasted with certainty, and would equal the affirmation of certitude. In this case Newman would be using 'divine faith' to refer to what we have been calling an affirmation of certitude.

Thus far, we can conclude that when Newman uses the concept 'act of will' to refer to a decision (rather than to personal intellectual appropriation) he could mean either of two things. We considered the first — an affirmation or commitment to human certitude — in the previous chapter. So far in this chapter, we have seen that it could also refer to the act of divine faith. Ambiguity, therefore, in some of the texts has raised the problem of the relation of the affirmation to the act of divine faith, generating the question whether or not the act of divine faith is coextensive with the affirmation of human certainty, and precisely how divine faith would differ from human faith in each case.

There are several prima-facie reasons for concluding that Newman did in fact see divine faith as a distinct affirmation, through grace, of *fides acquisita,* over and above the affirmation we considered in earlier chapters; none of them, however, are conclusive.

First, Newman considered that divine faith was accompanied by a higher degree of certainty than *fides acquisita.* In his *Essay on the Development of Doctrine* he noted with approval some remarks found in Huet's 'Essay on the Human Understanding':

men know God in two manners. By Reason, with entire human certainty; and by Faith, with absolute and divine certainty. . . . tis clear we cannot, neither in the natural knowledge we have of God, which is acquired by Reason, nor in science founded on geometrical principles and theorems, find absolute and consummate certainty, but only that

---

[7] *T.P.,* p. 7 (30 Apr. 1853); the arrow-brackets indicate Newman's own interlinear insertions.

human certainty . . . to which nevertheless every wise man ought to submit his understanding.[8]

Later, in his papers on certainty, Newman claimed that religious certainty, 'in any proper sense of the word', implies the highest degree of certainty — that is, not only the absence of all doubt but also the absence of fear.[9] In a subsequent paper, Newman claimed that this higher degree of certainty is not part of *fides acquisita*; the assent of *fides acquisita* is an assent without doubt but not without fear.[10]

This particular warrant for seeing divine faith as a decision over and above the decisions to affirm our certitude, however, must be qualified in two respects. First, after claiming that *fides acquisita* is not an assent without fear, Newman wrote at the end of the paper: 'Question — is not all doubt and fear excluded in our faith in the laws of nature?'[11] He had also noted earlier that the higher certainty is 'of usual occurrence'.[12] So Newman's distinction between *fides acquisita* and *fides divina* in terms of a higher certainty is not unproblematical for him. Secondly, and more importantly, it is not necessary that divine faith be a different affirmation in order to manifest a higher degree of certainty. The operation of grace might sufficiently account for that.

More significant warrant for the claim that Newman saw divine faith as not coextensive with the affirmation of human certitude is provided by the following remarks. In reminding us of the 'pre-eminence of strength in divine faith' (186), Newman notes that its 'intrinsic superiority' comes first from its 'differing from human faith, [not] merely in degree of assent, but in its being superior in nature and kind' (187, 186). He continues: in the assent which 'follows on a divine announcement, and is vivified by a divine grace, there is, from the nature of the case, a transcendent adhesion of the mind, intellectual and moral, and a special self-protection, beyond the operation of . . . ordinary laws of thought' (187). Newman's emphasis on 'divine announcement' refers to the

---

[8] *Dev.*, pp. 333–4.

[9] *T.P.*, p. 3 (Apr. 1853); cf. also pp. 4–5 (14 Apr. 1853) where it is explained that doubt concerns derivation of conclusion from premisses, whereas fear concerns the grounds themselves.   [10] *T.P.*, p. 37 (16 Dec. 1853).

[11] Ibid., p. 38.   [12] *T.P.*, p. 5 (14 Apr. 1853).

relation of faith to *testimony*; this is explicated further in a paper on certainty:

Fides divina, I suppose, has this difference from Fides humana, not only in its quality, but that fides, in the latter phrase, has something of a vague sense, and does not *necessarily* suppose a speaker.[13]

Divine faith is therefore personal in a way that religious belief is not.

One way of understanding what Newman means by this superior status or quality is suggested by his earliest account in the *Grammar* of the limits of his concern. In the passage referred to at the beginning of this chapter, Newman wrote that he was concerned with 'what it is to believe in [religious doctrines], what the mind does, what it contemplates, when it makes an act of faith' (99). He meant, however, 'not precisely faith, because faith, in its theological sense, includes a belief, not only in the thing believed, but also in the ground of believing; that is, not only belief in certain doctrines, but belief in them expressly because God has revealed them' (99–100). The material object, he suggests, is the same; divine faith, however, differs in terms of its formal object.

Newman distinguishes between divine and human faith, therefore, in terms of a distinction between formal and material object. I suggest that this reveals a great deal about his view of the relation of the affirmation of human certainty to divine faith, and the qualitatively superior status of divine faith. Since the material object is the same, divine and human faith are materially obverses of each other; the same material object is looked at from different perspectives. As he said in his letter to Mrs Froude, noted above, we can realize that faith is a divine gift, yet still talk about what the mind does — faith can be a grace-initiated and grace-supported decision to affirm our reasoning process.

Fey claims that sometimes, especially in his early *University Sermons,* Newman 'suggested that faith is a decision to act on a judgement of credibility and nothing more'.[14] Since Fey judges this to be equivalent to assuming that faith is simply an assent to an argument, he concludes that Newman later changed his position. On the contrary, I suggest that Newman

[13] *T.P.*, p. 38 (15 Dec. 1853).   [14] Fey, *Faith and Doubt,* p. 59, n. 70.

need not have changed. Faith could be a decision to affirm the certainty we experience, but a decision informed by grace, and resulting in a consummate certainty qualitatively distinct from the earlier one. It is possible for divine faith to maintain its distinctiveness without having to be seen as a separate affirmation or decision. Divine faith differs from human faith in being an affirmation through grace, and in response to testimony, formally different albeit materially the same as *fides acquisita*. Accordingly, the affirmation we have considered in earlier chapters would be part of *fides acquisita* in those cases in which grace did not operate or was not necessary, and part of *fides divina* where it was a response to grace, affirming the beliefs 'expressly because God revealed them'.

It is not surprising that Newman's view of the divine gift of faith is not easily determinable. First, any attempt to explain a 'divine' phenomenon is clearly subject to difficulties not inherent in an explication of a purely natural one. Secondly, Newman tended to see grace as influencing all our actions in some sense, so he did not always distinguish carefully between divine and human faith.[15] In the preceding examination, therefore, I have set out the possible relations between divine faith and the affirmation of human certainty suggested by the ambiguity in several of Newman's claims about 'the act of the will'.

Newman's own view of the material identity of the object of religious belief and divine faith, and their formal difference, warrants the conclusion that the distinctive quality of divine faith, as he saw it in terms of grace, testimony, and the particular certainty with its 'transcendent adhesion' and 'special self-protection', did not require that divine faith be an affirmation over and above the affirmation of certitude we considered in earlier chapters. Further confirmation is found in the following passage, which 'dovetails' with this conclusion in all respects:

the peculiar nature of divine faith . . . cannot be treated as an ordinary conviction or belief. Faith is a gift of God, and not a mere act of our own, which we are free to exert when we will. It is quite distinct

[15] Ibid., pp. 38–9.

from an exercize of reason, though it follows upon it. . . . I may see that I ought to believe and yet be unable to believe. . . . Now faith is not a mere conviction in reason, it is a firm assent, it is a clear certainty greater than any other certainty; and this is wrought in the mind by the grace of God . . . alone. As then men may be convinced and not act according to their conviction, so they may be convinced and not believe according to their conviction.[16]

It is, moreover, likely that Newman saw the act of divine faith as coextensive not merely with the active confirmation of religious belief, but with the role of the will within the reasoning process itself in coming to certitude. In his letter to Mrs Ward, Newman discussed the role of the will 'as moved by grace or not'. He claimed that although we 'see on the whole that the grounds are sufficient for conviction', 'this is not the same thing as conviction'.[17] His explanation is that 'if conviction were unavoidable we might be said to be forced to believe, as we are forced to believe mathematical conclusions — but while there is enough evidence for conviction, whether we *will* be convinced or not rests with ourselves'. The 'willing' Newman is speaking of here, as possible through grace, is either the affirmation of certitude or the willing involved in personal reasoning. In either case, his emphasis is on the opposition of impersonal compulsion to personal conviction.

He refers in the same letter, by way of further explanation, to his novel *Loss and Gain,* where the priest answers the question what is to make a man believe, by saying 'his will'.[18] But if one turns to *Loss and Gain,* one sees that the priest is saying that when the evidence is not 'enough to *subdue* the reason', what will make him believe is 'the *will*, his *will*'.[19] And we see from the priest's further words that this simply means that the evidence 'requires to be brought home or applied to the mind'.[20] It is clear that he is again speaking of the willing involved in personal intellectual appropriation of non-demonstrative conclusions.

[16] *Mix. I,* 'Faith and Doubt', p. 225.

[17] *L.D.,* 12:289 (12 Oct. 1848). Cf. Newman's next letter to Mrs Ward, however, in which he discussed the case as one in which 'your intellect is convinced, but in *spite* of that conviction, you are haunted with doubts', *L.D.,* 12:356 (30 Nov. 1848).

[18] Ibid. [19] *L.G.,* p. 384. [20] Ibid.

Grace, therefore, can, for Newman, be considered as capable of influencing the entire process, the willing both during and after the reasoning, resulting in consummate certainty. This is, no doubt, what he means by claiming that instead of it being true that Reason warrants and *then* Faith embraces, 'the act of Faith is sole and elementary'.[21]

Before turning to a consideration of the relation of divine faith to the adherence of religious belief, it is worthwhile to point out the value of the conclusions drawn thus far by looking at a claim made in a recent account of Newman's thought — a claim which can be clearly recognized as misleading in light of the preceding discussion. Although providing an important and well-documented reminder of the variety of contexts of discourse in Newman's thought, Jouett Powell makes a claim which illustrates the imprecision which often surrounds judgements concerning the role of the will in Newman's thought.[22] Powell writes: 'The element of will is a safeguard against the equation of *fides acquisita* and *fides divina*.'[23] The element of will provides the distinction between the two, because, as Powell claimed earlier, human faith is an 'act of the will' while divine faith is a gift of grace.[24]

We have seen, however, that the 'element of will' can refer to a number of different things for Newman, none of which unproblematically differentiates *fides divina* from *fides acquisita*. First, we saw that there is no simple 'act of will'. The 'element of will' in *fides acquisita* can refer to the personal intellectual appropriation involved in reaching certitude. It can also refer to the 'element of will' in the affirmation of certitude which Newman saw as necessary in the face of intellectual and moral weakness.

Our inquiry in this chapter, moreover, led to the conclusion that there was ambiguity concerning an 'element of will' in divine faith. Either it was coextensive with the affirmation of certitude or it was a further affirmation distinct from it. In neither case would the 'element of will' provide a distinction between *fides acquisita* and *fides divina* in the way Powell

---

[21] *U.S.*, 'The Nature of Faith in Relation to Reason', p. 202.
[22] *Three Uses of Christian Discourse in John Henry Newman.*
[23] Ibid., p. 108.   [24] Ibid., p. 39.

suggests. Either there was one and the same act of will in both, or they each involve decisions; the 'element of will' does not, therefore, 'safeguard against the equation' of the two. Our conclusion that Newman saw the 'act of divine faith' as coextensive with the 'act of will' in some or all of its manifestations reveals the misleading imprecision in a claim like Powell's. Although a grace-less 'act of will' can be contrasted with a grace-full one, no simple opposition of an 'act of will' to a gift of grace can be made.

2. Adherence – Religious Belief and Divine Faith

It should be clear as a result of the preceding chapters that there is a strand in Newman's thought according to which the doubt Newman saw as incompatible with religious certitude did not preclude rational openness to criticism. Newman's claim that doubt is incompatible with the certitude necessary for faith resolved itself into three kinds of admissions concerning doubt:

(1) admissions concerning the fallibility and logical incompleteness of concrete reasoning – these however, do not constitute genuine dubitability;

(2) admissions concerning the kind of doubt that is compatible with certainty – i.e. the admission of genuine dubitability (of doubt which is theoretically possible, but not reasonable in this particular case);

(3) admissions concerning the kind of doubt that is not compatible with certainty – i.e. suspension of assent or certitude, admission that the doubt is reasonable in this case, admission that only practical certitude is attainable, admission that fear, hesitation, or reservation is reasonable.

Since I have been considering religious certitude in the *Grammar* these conclusions are directed to this kind of certitude. It might now be objected that they have nothing to do with Newman's view of divine faith, since it exhibits a 'transcendent adhesion' and 'special self-protection' which does not operate in the course of ordinary belief.

Soon after his conversion Newman saw the need to answer similar objections raised against Catholicism. As we pointed out earlier Newman considered the criticism that those who become Catholics are forbidden to 'reconsider' the question of divine authority. Critics mean by reconsideration, he said, 'an inquiry springing from doubt of it, and possibly ending in a denial'.[25] Critics argue that 'once a Catholic, he never, never can doubt again; that, whatever his misgivings may be, he must stifle them, nay must start from them as the suggestions of the evil spirit; in short, that the must give up altogether the search after truth, and do a violence to his mind, which is nothing short of immoral'.[26]

This same objection was considered by Newman in an 1860 paper on the 'popular, practical and personal evidence for the truth of revelation'.[27] Since the great mass of Catholics do not reason to their faith, but receive it 'by inheritance' and cultivate it in 'contracted' course of study, their faith, it is objected, is not rational. Catholics are told

they must take care to be certain it is true, and to force themselves into a sustained pitch of certainty by the action of their will, if they begin to lag, and to repress as poison any doubt or any desire fairly to consider such various aspects of the subject, such as new fields of argument, as are at a later time proffered to their consideration.[28]

This is not rational belief, it is claimed, but rather a 'persuasion which [a Catholic] does not like to have disturbed'.

W. G. Ward, attempting to defend the *Grammar* from its Catholic critics, vividly summarized the position of the philosophical critic of Catholicism. The latter considers that the Church prescribes 'a rebellion against reason'.[29] Since the Church refuses to allow Catholics to suspend their judgement on the truth of Catholicism until they have demonstrative proof, the philosophical critic can only conclude that the intellectual maxims of Catholics put them beyond the 'pale of intellectual civilization'; these maxims allow as much rational intercourse with them as with a 'savage'.

Do these traditional objections against the immunization of faith against criticism, first enunciated by Newman's contemporaries and then reiterated by philosophers like Bartley, still hold with respect to divine faith? Does the 'transcendent adhesion' of divine faith mean that, unlike the certitude we considered, divine certitude results in or requires a rebellion

---

[25] *Mix. I,* 'Faith and Doubt', p. 215.   [26] Ibid.
[27] *T.P.,* pp. 81–9 (5 Jan. 1860).   [28] Ibid., pp. 81–2.
[29] Ward II, pp. 271–2.

against reason in the form of an indefeasible obligation to maintain certitude 'come what may'? In what follows I want to argue that a parallel can be drawn between the kind of all-or-nothing adherence I have proposed as normative in Newman's view of religious certitude, and the kind of adherence involved in the consummate certainty of divine faith.

Indirect support for the claim that the adherence Newman saw as necessary in divine faith would not have been, if worked out, significantly different from that which we have described in relation to the religious certitude of the *Grammar* can be found in Newman's view of the relation of the natural to the supernatural. Newman's whole method in the *Grammar* indicates that he saw an understanding of religious belief as dependent on an understanding of belief and certitude in general. In particular, Newman discusses the relation of natural and revealed faith at the end of the *Grammar,* making the following provocative comment:

Instead of saying that the truths of Revelation depend on those of Natural Religion, it is more pertinent to say that belief in revealed truths depends on belief in natural. . . . Belief generates belief; states of mind correspond to each other; the habits of thought and the reasonings which lead us on to a higher state of belief than our present, are the very same which we already possess in connexion with the lower state. (413)

States of mind correspond with each other; habits of thought, therefore, will not be radically different in the natural and supernatural realm.

Boekraad, commenting on this same passage in Newman, claims that Newman thereby recognized that it would be vain to 'attempt a solution of the problem on the supernatural level without any reference to the parallel problem on the natural plane'.[30] Newman, continues Boekraad:

considers the solution of the natural or philosophical problem . . . as an indispensable guidance in the solution of the same problem in the supernatural sphere. *We can therefore consider the former as the very basis for the solution of the problem in its entire complexity,* that is in regard to both natural and supernatural truth.[31]

Boekraad here elaborates what I take to be a correct view of

---

[30] Boekraad, *The Personal Conquest of Truth,* pp. 34–5.
[31] Ibid., p. 35, italics mine.

Newman's understanding of the relation of natural and supernatural in this respect. It is at least plausible, therefore,
that Newman could have seen a model of commitment appropriate to religious certainty at the level of human belief as the
basis for an understanding of the adherence of divine faith.

Even more direct warrant for that claim can be found in
several of Newman's texts, some of which we have already
considered in coming to our understanding of the adherence
proposed in the *Grammar*. Many of the conclusions I presented concerning the dubitability and corrigibility which
Newman saw as compatible with religious certitude were in
fact based on texts in which Newman was clearly, sometimes
even explicitly, referring to divine faith.

As an Anglican Newman had written in the *Via Media*
(1837) that doubt was an inherent part of faith, or at least
compatible with it.[32] In his Catholic emendations in 1871
Newman corrected this claim, qualifying what was meant by
doubt. He claimed that earlier he meant by 'doubt' a 'recognition of the logical incompleteness of its proof, not a refusal
to pronounce it true. Both Catholics and Anglicans doubt
more or less in the former sense, neither of them doubt in
the latter'.[33] The doubt that is incompatible cannot 'be anything short of a deliberate withholding of assent to the
Church's teaching'.[34] A 'sense of imperfection or incompleteness in the argumentative grounds of religion' is not incompatible with faith.[35] Thus the possibility of admitting our
fallibility, and the corrigibility of all human beliefs which we
saw to be compatible with religious certitude, seems equally
compatible with divine faith. What is incompatible with the
latter as well as with the former is the claim that it is reasonable to doubt in this particular case, i.e. the withholding or
suspension of assent.

We can refer again to Newman's *Discourses to Mixed Congregations,* 'Faith and Doubt', where he offers a similar
commentary on the doubt that is incompatible with certainty.
'Take an instance', he says: 'what would you think of a
friend whom you loved, who could bargain that, in spite of

---

[32] *V.M. I*, p. 87.   [33] Ibid., p. 108, n.2.
[34] Ibid., p. 85, n. 4.   [35] Ibid.

his present trust in you, he might be allowed some day to doubt you?'[36] Newman suggests that if a man professes certainty, and then adds that 'for what he knew, he might doubt one day about' what he now claims to be certain of, such a man is not certain. On the contrary, 'such an anticipa-tion would be a real, though latent, doubt, betraying that he was not certain of it at present'.[37] What Newman is claiming here is that such an admission is effectively a recognition of the reasonableness of doubt in the case at hand, and this is clearly incompatible with certainty and faith: 'He who really believes in it now, cannot imagine the future discovery of reasons to shake his faith.'[38] Certainty implies the believer's claim that he is sure that what in future might appear to be negative evidence will in fact be 'neutralizable', capable of being reinterpreted. The incompatibility of doubt in this sense, however, does not require dogmatism.[39]

We noted earlier that the independence of assent from inference did not require that assent be uninfluenced by variations in the inferential warrants. One of the texts to which we referred earlier suggested that this independence might be accounted for by the fact that the assent could not be resolved into the inferential warrants: 'assent does not really depend on those *motiva*, for no conclusion can be more certain than the premises from which it is drawn. In other words, it is not resolvable into its *motiva*'.[40] What should be noted here, however, is that Newman is referring explicitly in this case to the assent of divine faith, i.e. 'Faith [as] a *firm assent* to the word of God *obscurely revealed*'.[41] Thus, the independence of the assent of divine faith from the reasoning involved is similar to the independence of human certitude from its reasons. That independence, as we saw, did not in principle preclude the possibility of criticism, and even abandonment of the certitude. I suggest that it need not, in principle, preclude it in the case of divine faith either.

If it is true that the kind of doubt that is incompatible with faith and the kind that is compatible are not significantly

[36] *Mix. I*, 'Faith and Doubt', p. 219.   [37] Ibid., p. 216.   [38] Ibid., p. 219.
[39] Cf. George Dicker, 'Certainty without Dogmatism' (Chap. V, n. 36).
[40] 'On the Nature and Cause of Faith', 1848, cited by Pailin, *The Way to Faith*, Appendix III, p. 208.   [41] Ibid.

different from what is the case in religious certitude, then it would not be surprising to find that the criticizability and possibility of abandonment might be significantly the same. This is precisely the case, I suggest, as is clear from a consideration of two passages which we have considered already, although without emphasizing the fact that they concerned divine faith. In a paper of 27 March 1860, Newman sketched an outline for a book he was planning. Chapter 4 concerned the 'mode in which the mass of persons thus brought to faith [by popular, personal motiva], should bear themselves towards objections to revelation. Should they allow themselves fairly to examine? I say, yes, if it *comes* in their way and they have a duty to do so.'[42] By describing the kind of doubt that was compatible and claiming that they could consider objections 'fairly', Newman met the objections that Catholics must 'repress as poison any doubt or any desire fairly to consider' new information offered to them. Chapter 5, moreover, suggests the kind of adherence appropriate to divine faith:

On revelation being directed to a person and devotional and how this affects the question. You may examine with your *will* determinatedly fixed. As when a friend is accused, you do not let yourself doubt him *at all,* till he is found guilty.[43]

Newman's caution that we must be sure that God is '*such* a friend', i.e. that we are really related to him in genuine devotion, or we may be led astray by investigation, does not negate the import of this passage. Adherence is necessarily of a certain mode, but it can be abandoned. That doubt is judged incompatible with faith does not make Newman's believer a rebel against reason, but it does ensure that he adheres long enough to do justice to the personal relation involved.

I have concluded that there is sufficient warrant for a claim that the adherence Newman saw as appropriate to divine faith is significantly similar in relevant respects to the adherence that is appropriate to the religious certitude of the *Grammar*. In neither case does certitude or sufficient adherence result from or require a rebellion against reason.

---

[42] *T.P.*, p. 91 (27 Mar. 1860).   [43] Ibid.

This conclusion is indirectly an explication of a claim by Lee Yearley that in order to do justice to Newman's thought, the notion of two distinct spheres — a natural and a revealed — must be replaced by 'the idea of one religious sphere containing various distinctions'.[44] Genuine religious faith is a totally grace-informed process of coming to see God as revealing and revealed. There is one religious sphere, not two realms. In this Newman shows himself a genuine descendent of that theological tradition in which grace does not simply add to or replace nature, but intensifies and perfects it.

[44] Lee Yearley, *The Ideas of Newman: Christianity and Human Religiosity* (University Park: Penn State University Press, 1978), p. 3. I received Mr Yearley's book too late for me to take account of his more specific conclusions in this respect.

Selected Bibliography

The following is a list of only those works cited. For a complete listing of Newman's works and works on Newman, consult *Newman-Studien*, edited by Werner Becker and Heinrich Fries (Nürnberg: Glock und Lutz).

A. JOHN HENRY NEWMAN

Apologia Pro Vita Sua. Edited by Martin J. Svaglic. Oxford: Clarendon Press, 1967.

Cardinal Newman and William Froude, FRS: A Correspondence. Edited by Gordon Huntington Harper. Baltimore: Johns Hopkins Press, 1933.

Discourses Addressed to Mixed Congregations. 6th ed. London; Burns & Oates, 1881. Vol. I.

An Essay in Aid of a Grammar of Assent. London: Longman, Green & Co., 1901.

An Essay on the Development of Christian Doctrine. New Edition. London: Basil Montagu Pickering, 1878.

Essays Critical and Historical. Vol. I. 2nd ed. London: Basil Montague Pickering, 1872.

The Idea of a University, Defined and Illustrated. Edited and Introduced by Martin J. Svaglic. New York and London, 1960.

John Henry Newman: Autobiographical Writings. Edited by Henry Tristram. New York: Sheed & Ward, 1957.

The Letters and Diaries of John Henry Newman. Introduction and notes by Charles Stephen Dessain (*et al.*). Vols. 11–18. London: Thomas Nelson and Sons, Ltd., 1961–8.

Loss and Gain. The Story of a Convert. 6th ed. London: Burns, Oates & Co., 1874.

Newman's University Sermons: Fifteen Sermons Preached Before University of Oxford 1826–43, 3rd ed. (1871). Edited by D. M. MacKinnon and J. D. Holmes. London: S.P.C.K., 1970.

Philosophical Readings in Cardinal Newman. Edited by James Collins. Chicago: Henry Regnery, 1961.

The Theological Papers of John Henry Newman on Faith and Certainty. Edited by Hugo Achaval and J. Derek Holmes, with Introduction by C. S. Dessain. Oxford: Clarendon Press, 1976.

The Via Media of the Anglican Church. Vol. 1: Lectures on the Prophetical Office of the Church, Viewed Relatively to Romanism and Popular Protestantism. London: Longmans, Green & Co., 1911.

B. OTHER WORKS: BOOKS

Aaron, Richard. *Knowing and the Function of Reason.* Oxford: Clarendon Press, 1971.

Armstrong, D. M. *Belief, Truth and Knowledge.* Cambridge: University Press, 1973.

Bambrough, Renford. *Reason, Truth and God.* London: Methuen, 1969.

Barbour, Ian. *Myths, Models and Paradigms.* New York: Harper & Row, 1974.

Barth, Karl. *Evangelical Theology: An Introduction.* Trans. by Grover Foley. New York: Holt, Rinehart & Winston, 1963.

Bartley, William W. *Retreat to Commitment.* New York: Alfred A. Knopf, 1962.

Boekraad, A. J. *The Personal Conquest of Truth According to J. H. Newman.* Louvain: Editions Nauwelaerts, 1955.

Bultmann, Rudolf. *Jesus Christ and Mythology.* New York: Scribner's, 1958.

_____. *Kerygma and Myth.* Edited by Hans Werner Bartsch. New York: Harper Torchbooks, 1961.

Cameron, J. M. *The Night Battle: Essays.* London: The Catholic Book Club, 1962.

Chadwick, Owen, ed. *The Mind of the Oxford Movement.* Stanford, Calif.: Stanford University Press, 1960.

Christian, William. *Meaning and Truth in Religion.* Princeton: Princeton University Press, 1964.

Cockshut, A. O. J. *The Unbelievers: English Agnostic Thought.* London: Collins, 1964.

Collins, James. Introduction to *Philosophical Readings in Cardinal Newman.* Chicago: Henry Regnery, 1961.

Coulson, John. *Newman and the Common Tradition.* Oxford: Clarendon Press, 1970.

D'Arcy, M. C. *The Nature of Belief.* London: Sheed & Ward, 1931.

Fey, William R. *Faith and Doubt: The Unfolding of Newman's Thought on Certainty.* Shepherdstown, W.Va.: Patmos Press, 1976.

Flew, Antony. *God and Philosophy.* New York: Delta Bks., Dell Publ., 1966.

Hacker, P. M. S. *Insight and Illusion.* Oxford: Clarendon Press, 1972.

Hacking, Ian. *The Emergence of Probability.* Cambridge: The University Press, 1975.

Hampshire, Stuart. *Thought and Action.* London: Chatto & Windus, 1959.

Harman, Gilbert. *Thought.* Princeton, N.J.: Princeton University Press, 1973.

Hume, David. *Enquiry Concerning Human Understanding.* Edited by Eric Steinberg. Indianapolis: Hackett Publ. Co., 1977.

Hutton, Richard H. *Cardinal Newman.* Cambridge: The Riverside Press, 1890.

Kiesler, Charles A. *The Psychology of Commitment.* New York: Academic Press, 1971.

Lakatos, Imre and Musgrave, Alan, eds. *Criticism and the Growth of Knowledge*. Cambridge: University Press, 1970.

Lehrer, Keith. *Knowledge*. Oxford: Clarendon Press, 1974.

Livingston, James C. *The Ethics of Belief: An Essay on the Victorian Religious Conscience*. AAR Studies in Religion 9. Tallahassee, Fla.: American Academy of Religion and Scholars' Press, 1974.

Locke, John. *An Essay Concerning Human Understanding*. 2 vols. New York: Dover Publications, 1959.

MacIntyre, Alasdair, ed. *Metaphysical Beliefs*. London: SCM Press, 1957.

MacIntyre, Alasdair and Ricoeur, Paul. *The Religious Significance of Atheism*. Bampton Lectures 18, 1966. New York and London: Columbia University Press, 1969.

Mavrodes, George. *Belief in God*. Studies in Philosophy. New York: Random House, 1970.

Middleton, R. D. *Newman at Oxford*. London: Oxford University Press, 1950.

Mitchell, Basil. *The Justification of Religious Belief*. New York: Seabury Press, 1973.

Moore, G. E. *Philosophical Papers*. London: Allen & Unwin Ltd., 1959.

Morawetz, Thomas. *Wittgenstein and Knowledge*. Amherst, Mass.: University of Massachusetts Press, 1978.

Pailin, David. *The Way to Faith: An Examination of Newman's 'Grammar of Assent' as a Response to the Search for Certainty in Faith*. London: Epworth Press, 1969.

Peirce, Charles S. *Selected Writings*. Edited by Philip Weiner, New York: Dover Publ., 1958.

Polanyi, Michael. *Personal Knowledge*. Chicago: University of Chicago Press, 1962.

Powell, Jouett Lynn. *Three Uses of Christian Discourse in John Henry Newman: An Example of Non-reductive Reflection on the Christian Faith*. Dissertation Series, No. 10. Missoula, Montana: Scholars' Press, 1975.

Price, H. H. *Belief* (Gifford Lectures of 1960). Muirhead Library of Philosophy Series. London: George Allen & Unwin Ltd., 1969.

Quine, Willard Van Orman. *From a Logical Point of View*. New York: Harper Torchbooks, 1963.

Quine, W. V. O. and Ullian, J. S. *The Web of Belief*. New York: Random House, 1970.

Reardon, Bernard M. G. *Religious Thought in the Nineteenth Century*. Cambridge: Cambridge University Press, 1966.

Sherry, Patrick. *Religion, Truth and Language Games*. New York: Macmillan, 1977.

Stephen, Leslie. *An Agnostic's Apology*. New York: G.P. Putnam's Sons, London: Smith, Elder, 1893.

Tillich, Paul. *Dynamics of Faith*. New York: Harper Torchbooks, 1957.

———. *The Protestant Era*. Chicago: University of Chicago Press, 1957 (abr. ed.).

Van Leeuwen, Henry. *The Problem of Certainty in English Thought 1630–1690.* The Hague: Martinus Nijhoff, 1963.

Vargish, Thomas. *Newman: The Contemplation of Mind.* Oxford: Clarendon Press, 1970.

Walgrave, Jan H. *Newman the Theologian.* Translated by A. V. Littledale. New York: Sheed & Ward, 1960.

Ward, Wilfred. *Life of John Henry Cardinal Newman.* Vols. I and II. New York: Longman, Green & Co., 1912.

Weatherby, Harold. *Cardinal Newman in His Age.* Nashville: Vanderbilt University Press, 1973.

Whately, Richard. *Elements of Logic.* New York: William Jackson, 1832.

White, Alan R. *Modal Thinking.* Ithaca: Cornell University Press, 1975.

Wisdom, John. *Paradox and Discovery.* Berkeley: University of California Press, 1970.

Wittgenstein, Ludwig. *On Certainty.* Edited by G. E. M. Anscombe and G. H. von Wright. Translated by Denis Paul and G. E. M. Anscombe. New York: Harper & Row, 1969.

_____. *Philosophical Investigations.* 3rd ed. Translated by G. E. M. Anscombe. New York: Macmillan Co., 1968.

Yearley, Lee. *The Ideas of Newman: Christianity and Human Religiosity.* University Park: Penn State University Press, 1978.

Zeno. Dr., OFM Cap. *John Henry Newman, Our Way to Certitude:* An Introduction to Newman's Psychological Discovery: The Illative Sense and His *Grammar of Assent.* Leiden: E. J. Brill, 1957.

C. OTHER WORKS: ARTICLES

Aiken, Henry. 'Honesty and Commitment: The Philosopher's View.' In *Intellectual Honesty and Religious Commitment.* Edited by Arthur Bellinzoni and Thomas Litzenburg. Philadelphia: Fortress Press, 1969.

Alston, William. 'Unconscious Intellectual Dishonesty in Religion.' In *Intellectual Honesty and Religious Commitment.* Edited by Arthur Bellinzoni and Thomas Litzenburg. Philadelphia: Fortress Press, 1969.

Austin, William. 'Religious Commitment and the Logical Status of Doctrines.' *Religious Studies* 9 (March 1973).

Barker, Stephen. 'Must Every Inference Be Either Deductive Or Inductive?' In *Philosophy in America.* Muirhead Library of Philosophy. Edited by Max Black. Ithaca: Cornell University Press, 1965.

Beer, John. 'Newman and the Romantic Sensibility.' In *The English Mind.* Edited by Hugh Sykes Davies and George Watson. Cambridge: University Press, 1964.

Brunton, J. A. 'The Indefectibility of Certitude.' *Downside Review* 86 (July 1968).

Clifford, William K. 'The Ethics of Belief.' In *Lectures and Reviews,* vol. II. London: Macmillan, 1901.

Dessain, Charles Stephen. 'Cardinal Newman on the Theory and Practice of Knowledge. The Purpose of the Grammar of Assent.' *Downside Review* 75 (January 1957).

Dicker, George. 'Certainty Without Dogmatism: A Reply to Unger's "An Argument for Skepticism".' *Philosophical Exchange* 1 (Summer 1974).

Encyclopedia of Philosophy, reprint ed. 1972. S.v. 'Certainty', by C. D. Rollins; 'Choosing, Deciding and Doing', by Andrew Oldenquist; 'Doubt', by Harry G. Frankfurt.

Greenlea, Douglas. 'Unrestricted Fallibilism.' *Trans. C. S. Peirce Society* (April 1971).

Hudson, W. D. 'Professor Bartley's Theory of Rationality and Religious Commitment.' *Religious Studies* 9 (September 1973).

Hunter, J. F. M. 'Forms of Life in Wittgenstein's *Philosophical Investigations.*' *American Philosophical Quarterly* 5 (October 1968).

James, William. 'The Will to Believe.' In *The Will to Believe: Human Immortality*. New York: Dover Publ. Inc., 1956.

Ker, I. T. 'Recent Critics of Newman's *Grammar.*' *Religious Studies* 13 (March 1977).

Malcolm, Norman. 'Knowledge and Belief.' In *Knowledge and Belief*. Edited by A. Phillips Griffiths. Oxford: Oxford University Press, 1967.

Marty, Martin. 'Religious Commitment and Rational Criticism.' *Philosophical Forum* 2 (Fall 1970).

Maurice, F. D. 'Dr. Newman's *Grammar of Assent.*' *The Contemporary Review* 14 (May 1870).

Mayo. Bernard. 'Belief and Constraint.' In *Knowledge and Belief*. Edited by A. Phillips Griffiths.

Mooney, Edward F. 'Assertion and Commitment in Religious Belief.' *Sophia* 10 (April 1971).

Naulty, R. A. 'Newman's Dispute with Locke.' *Journal of the History of Philosophy* 11 (October 1973).

Newman, Jay. 'Cardinal Newman's Phenomenology of Religious Belief.' *Religious Studies* 10 (June 1974).

Pojman, Louis. 'Belief and Will.' *Religious Studies* 14 (March 1978).

Price, H. H. 'Belief and Will.' *Proceedings of the Aristotelian Society Supplement* 28 (1954).

Rudinow, Joel. 'Religious Commitment I.' *Sophia* 12 (April, 1973).

Sherry, Patrick. 'Is Religion a "Form of Life"?' *American Philosophical Quarterly* 9 (April 1972).

Solomon, Robert C. 'God and Rationality.' *Canadian Journal of Philosophy* 4 (December 1974).

Stephen, Fitzjames. 'On Certitude in Religious Assent.' *Frazer's Magazine* (January 1872).

Thomson, Judith Jarvis, 'Reasons and Reasoning.' In *Philosophy in America.* Edited by Max Black. Ithaca: Cornell University Press, 1965.

Unger, Peter. 'An Argument for Skepticism.' *Philosophical Exchange* 1 (Summer 1974).

White, Alan R. 'On Claiming to Know.' In *Knowledge and Belief.* Edited by A. Phillips Griffiths.

Williams, Bernard. 'Deciding to Believe.' In *Problems of the Self.* Cambridge: At the University Press, 1973.

Wisdom, John. 'Gods.' In *Religious Language and the Problem of Religious Knowledge.* Edited by Ronald E. Santoni. Bloomington: Indiana University Press, 1968.

Woozley, A. D. 'Knowing and Not Knowing.' In *Knowledge and Belief.* Edited by A. Phillips Griffiths.

Zvara, Andrew. 'On Claiming to Know and Feeling Sure.' *Philosophical Studies* 24 (July 1973).

D. ANONYMOUS REVIEWS OF NEWMAN'S GRAMMAR

The Biblical Repertory and Princetown Review (April 1871).
The Edinburgh Review 132 (1870).

E. UNPUBLISHED WORKS

Dolan, Robert Rex. 'An Analysis of Religious Commitment.' Ph.D. dissertation, Columbia University, 1955.

Farley, Margaret. 'A Study in the Ethics of Commitment Within the Context of Theories of Human Love and Temporality.' Ph.D. dissertation, Yale University, 1973.

Morton, Adam. 'Our Knowledge of Theory.'

Index